Love Goddesses
of the Movies

Love Goddesses

Roger Manwell

of the Movies

Crescent Books

NEW YORK

This edition is published by
Crescent Books, a division of Crown Publishers, Inc.,
by arrangement with the Hamlyn Group.
Manufactured in Great Britain

Copyright
© The Hamlyn Publishing Group Limited MCMLXXV

Library of Congress Catalog Card No: 75-595
ISBN 0-517-131285

CONTENTS

The love goddesses pictured
in the endpapers
and preliminary pages are:
endpapers Rita Hayworth
half-title Greta Garbo
title page Betty Grable
this page Jeanne Moreau

INTRODUCTION

It might appear easy to choose 20 or so star actresses of the international cinema from its beginnings to the present time, the key films of which, in one way or another, have been about the relationships and complications of love. But it is not so easy as it appears. The film is over three-quarters of a century old, and actresses achieving world fame have starred in it since the teens of the century. The vast majority of films made have featured either love or action (adventure, war, the chase, domestic intrigue, and so on) and quite often both at once, told in romantic, dramatic, or melodramatic terms, so the range of choice on which to draw is formidable – in effect, the greater part of cinema. The actresses I have chosen, therefore, to represent the 'star image' in each decade since the 1910s have to fulfil many different conditions and possess many different qualities that give them special significance in comparison with others of their time – at least in my view.

This inevitably leads to some consideration of the broad social attitude to women held during the whole period involved, from 1910 or thereabouts, to the 1970s. For a film star to become universally acclaimed and admired (or perhaps abused) not only in her own but in other countries, she must be at once representative and unique. What is representative about her conforms to the current idea of what an attractive woman should be like; in this sense she belongs to the social 'climate' of her time, a climate which is all the while, year by year, shifting and evolving; what is unique about her is her own particular personality, the way she speaks, her individual looks and qualities of facial expression, her physical appearance, style and manner, her attitude to men and to other women, and so forth.

Her beauty – if indeed she is beautiful, as distinct from being exceptionally attractive, a difference which arises often – is, like her clothes, very much a creation of her time. In this she virtually has to be representative, however much she may manage to adapt or tone current styles to suit her private taste. In this a star's individual personality counts for a great deal; some accept a considerable degree of moulding by the stylists and the so-called 'charm schools', while others resist – Garbo was exceptionally strong in this respect. But in almost all cases there is a degree of conformity by the stars to the generally accepted pattern of hair-styling and costume of the period, however much their particular styles may modify what is general to women of their age-group, either simplifying or elaborating current trends. The film industry itself, so closely geared to fashion as part of its audience appeal, brings exceptional pressure to bear, in this, as in other respects, on its women stars, and nothing is more closely geared to its period than yesterday's film. Even historical costume is normally restyled in a contemporary fashion, giving it a supplementary style which can change with the period when the film was made.

But beyond this characteristic – the shift in appearance which takes place year by year in the stars of the past – lie the social values and attitudes the films themselves reflect. Each decade, in effect, produces its own thrust and counter-thrust in the attitude to and the attitude of women. The thrust is the standard to which conventional society tries to make its women conform; the counter-thrust is what women do more particularly to suit themselves, frequently in defiance of convention. Since films, like plays and novels, are concerned with situations involving conflict, the characters played by star actresses of strong personality usually reflect the counter-thrust, that is, they seem determined to get themselves into trouble. Women as a whole tend to be conformist, responding readily to the pattern of life, the values and conventions, society appears to approve for their age-group. The 'revolt' of the young against the behaviour-patterns of the middle aged is only a reflex kind of conformism to the new patterns set up by their own generation. Each generation also expects to find its particular values and attitudes faithfully reflected on the screen, indeed emphasized, exaggerated and idealized, with consequent dramatic clashes between the generations, and between those individual women who get into trouble and the society which is determined to oppose and, if necessary, punish them.

Each star has to find her own place in this network of social attitudes. If Mary Pickford (the first major woman star) aimed to be acceptable as the 'world's sweetheart' (a kind of 'girl next door' with exceptional verve and prettiness), this was scarcely the image of Garbo. While some might expect (in vain) to find Sophia Loren or Gina Lollobrigida or even Brigitte Bardot next door, the innate power of such enterprising 'personality' stars as Ingrid Thulin, Jeanne Moreau and Glenda Jackson (all inevitable counter-thrusters) place them in a new kind of category for female stardom, unique and memorable and nonconformist, but nevertheless in their own way the products of their age, as of course we all are. Others are nonconformist in a different way – Jean Harlow, Joan Crawford, Marilyn Monroe, Rita Hayworth – playing bad women as conventionally understood, exciting the sexuality in men without forming permanent or satisfying relationships, the kind of women established society condemns, while nevertheless finding them fascinating to watch in action on the screen.

We like (in fact) to use drama, novels, and fiction films to typify human nature, to discover its curiosities and eccentricities, to explore its heights and plumb its depravities. The extreme contemporary interest in crime, sexual irregularities and violence is largely exploration by people who have little desire or opportunity to practise these things themselves, but are nevertheless curious about them, since they represent behaviour known to be prevalent in certain sections of human society, and which were until comparatively recently only hinted at on the screen.

So, in choosing my range of stars I have had to keep all these various points in mind. Summarizing, I have had regard first of all to period, choosing admittedly very few stars from the silent era, and concentrating most of all on outstanding actresses from the 1930s to the present time because they seem to me to represent in their work, personality, style, and appearance the most significant values that have developed in screen stardom for women.

Secondly, I have kept in mind nationality, or national origin (which is not necessarily the same thing). My 19 stars are American, British, Swedish, Italian, French, and German, all internationally recognized and acclaimed. These stars all belong to the Western nations; I have not attempted to introduce the talented and beautiful women of the East (notably from India and Japan) who deserve a book of their own, since the cultures they represent are too divergent from ours. Although there have been considerable differences affecting the attitude to women and to the presentation of love on the screen in, say, the films of Sweden and Britain, these differences are largely a matter of degree and timing and do not represent any fundamental divergence in cultural values, which in all cases stem from the European tradition, a tradition which lies equally at the roots of society in North America.

Thirdly, I have tried to consider the general conception of beauty in women on the screen and what might be called their 'sexual mystique'. The convention of what makes up a beautiful appearance has obviously changed considerably from period to period, as each generation of stars, and their attendant cosmeticians, hairstylists and fashion-designers have vied to keep themselves in the forefront of a most lucrative business. A woman's face and hair may be remodelled annually to conform to the latest fashion in looks, and these detailed changes are both influenced by and in their turn influence the over-all appearance of the stars – though not necessarily some of those who figure in my primary selection.

In my view all those I have chosen are beautiful women in their own right. Whether they appear to conform exactly to the general conventions in beauty of their time or not, their primary quality is that they also possess the magic of 'sexual mystique', that is, they have depths of attraction which depend on personality, on the form of expression they adopt to life in general and the men of their choice. These women flower on the screen to an unusual degree, especially in response to men, and this makes them at once potent and vulnerable in sexual terms. Some modern stars possessing this attraction in depth are by no means beautiful in any conventional sense; if they are to be termed beautiful (as I think they should be) it is because of their capacity to reveal and express their feelings, their true femininity (in no old-fashioned, soft-centred meaning of the term). Just as a man possessing expressive, sensitive but highly irregular features can often appear more handsome than the conventionally handsome male, so an actress can be more beautiful than the conventionally pretty women (her lesser sisters of the screen) through the ability of her features constantly to reveal her inner emotional qualities.

Lastly, a certain number of stars have a special capacity to portray 'losers' – women who have a great need for love but who, for one reason or another, choose their men badly or with ill luck, and lose what they most hope to gain. The need for the portrayal of such situations reflects obviously a great romantic need in audiences, especially among women. The great love lost, the grand passion doomed to frustration often because it sins against social convention, has been a prime theme for romantic drama, mostly in the past, and stars of the varied sensitivity of Arletty, Ingrid Bergman, Monica Vitti and Glenda Jackson are all adept at the expression of such loss. It is part of the mystique in portraying love that it may well overleap what is possible, and the actress who specializes in portraying love relationships must know how to lose well.

The title given this book by the publishers might be thought ironic. The goddesses accepted rather than worshipped by the Greeks of classical times exhibited human traits, good and bad, which were no doubt more extravagant than those exhibited by normal humanity, but were nevertheless obviously conceived in the human image. The earlier film stars were, perhaps, goddesses in this somewhat debased classical sense, creating images which were both simpler and larger than life as it was represented by the millions of individual women who made up the vast international audiences gazing enrapt at the screen. But since the 1930s, with the arrival of the human voice in the cinema, women in films have become at once more complex and more natural (in the human sense) than the word 'goddess' implies, portraying characters who have drawn recognizably closer to the individual women who patronize the cinema.

The word 'goddess', therefore, becomes inappropriate to describe them; the stars have more recently become surrogates, or representative substitutes for the women who are their patrons and followers; they embody emotions of the kind these real women experience, or dream of experiencing, in a thousand varied situations devised for them by scriptwriters and directors. If the stars are 'worshipped' now it is for their transcendent looks, their skills, above all, perhaps, for their 'luck' in acquiring wealth, success and social acclaim (or opprobrium which makes them 'news'), while appearing to be little different in accent, manner, and even dress from ordinary women. It is the Cinderella syndrome over again, with far more of the fairy-story attached to it than a substitute for religious awe.

R. M.

THE BIRTH OF
THE STARS
1910-1919

It was not the film-producers who made the stars, it was their audiences. Very young, teenage actresses, sometimes with little or no training, but with ambitious parents, were the first regular female players on the popular screen. They had comparatively little to do, since the earliest story films were short one and two reelers, playing anything from 10, 20, or even on occasion 30 minutes in the period up to 1910, by which time the cinema had got through its early, teething period. It was beginning to establish itself as a form of entertainment which was more than a sideshow, and could sustain a full-length programme of entertainment of up to two hours. It was becoming worthy of its own theatres – the picture palaces and movie theatres which by 1910 were being established on a wide scale in many countries, and notably in America, Britain and France. The American, British and French companies pouring out films which were tending now to become much longer needed actors and actresses who were experienced enough to work fast in dumb-show and mime, and sustain performances in picture after picture which took, usually, only a few days to make. These players were paid very little before 1910, and their names did not appear on the screen or in the publicity

outside the cinemas. They were just known (for example) as the Biograph or the Vitagraph girls.

But their faces soon became familiar to the ever-growing number of film-goers. As their performances became more skilful, or more emphasized with the increasing length of the films and the demands made on them by the parts they played, so people began to ask who they were. The producers at first resisted this – they knew the inevitable result. The girls would get swell-headed and begin to demand more money. They might even become minor celebrities in their own right. Other producers might try to steal the better actresses away, bribing them with higher salaries. They were right. This was precisely what did happen. For example, one of the American Biograph girls was called Florence Lawrence, and her dark beauty began to attract considerable attention. The story is famous. Carl Laemmle, a rival producer, offered Miss Lawrence increased earnings, secured her services, and immediately gave her name away to the press. He then announced suddenly that she was dead. There was a sensation. Soon after, however, he announced with relief that she was, after all, still alive, and that it was envious rivals who had circulated the rumour of her death. There was another sensation. Ballyhoo was born, and the film trade press, already flourishing, established its ally in the fan magazines, which developed at the same time as the stars themselves when they became identified and began to achieve a measure of international celebrity. The new stars began to make 'personal appearances' to the delight of their fans, and to produce 'private lives' of some interest. At the same time they began to demand of their producers (or their mothers did for them) salaries which measured up to their new-found status and the social demands that went with it.

This kind of stardom was something entirely new in entertainment, like the films themselves. Stardom up to now had depended on cumulative appearances in theatre and vaudeville – you made yourself a star through years of success in performing in person before the public; for most this reputation was confined to their individual countries, though there had been much regular interchange of talent between Britain and America since the beginning of the

Lillian Gish, star created by D.W. Griffith in *Birth of a Nation* (1915) and *Intolerance* (1916).

19th century. Now international reputations could be made (seemingly) almost overnight by an impressive film performance which represented only a few days' work under the guidance of a skilled director like D.W. Griffith, a great maker of stars. Mere good looks and a pleasing manner in mime could give a girl a name internationally, since all films of any prominence achieved international circulation. Demands for prints grew with the reputation of the star in those parts of the world where there was hunger for films, and with the coming of the First World War the need for cheap and undemanding entertainment increased a thousandfold.

So stardom came for many: among the Americans, the Gish sisters (Lillian and Dorothy), Florence Turner, Mabel Normand (the comedienne who worked with Charlie Chaplin when he first appeared in films), Pearl White (the adventurous girl of the serials) and the exotic stars, Theda Bara and Alla Nazimova, but above all for Mary Pickford. In Britain, the stars included Alma Taylor, Chrissie White, and Ivy Close. Among the male stars, in addition to Chaplin, there were the dashing Douglas Fairbanks, Tom Mix, the handsome star of the Westerns, William S. Hart (originally a Shakespearean actor), William Farnum, and the stars of romantic drama, such as Francis X. Bushman and Earle Williams. For contrasting careers during the founding period of stardom for film actresses, it would be impossible to find greater divergence than in the careers of Mary Pickford, Theda Bara, and Gloria Swanson, whose true era began in the 1920s.

'Vamps, virgins and sweethearts are the archetypal trinity of the silent cinema,' Alexander Walker wrote in 'Sex and the Movies'. Once categorized, the early star actresses were, as we shall see, imprisoned in their own self-perpetuated image, often to the point of near-tragic immolation, like a good actor in the television series can become the prisoner of his success in the single role he is required to impersonate for years on end. This most certainly happened to both Mary Pickford and to Theda Bara during the days in which the nature of screen stardom was being established by the players and their public and their public images were being formed.

Mabel Normand, star of Mack Sennett's Keystone comedies from 1912.

Mary Pickford

For D.W. Griffith what mattered most in a girl he put before the camera was her 'soul'. 'I must have people with souls,' he said, 'people who know and feel their parts, and who express every single feeling in the entire gamut of emotions with their muscles. . . . It isn't what you do with your face or your hand, it's the light within.'

When Griffith (aged 33) first saw Mary Pickford (aged 16) at the studio, he was sufficiently struck by her curls to give her a screen test. It was 1909. She had no idea she was facing America's greatest film-maker; she did not even know his name, and if she had known it, it would have meant little to her. What experience had she had? he asked. Four years on the stage, she told him, adding with pride that two of them had been working for David Belasco. This name meant everything, since Belasco stood for Broadway and the height of theatrical achievement, whereas to work for the 'flickers' was more a disgrace than an achievement for an actress. 'You're too little and too fat', was Griffith's terse reaction, but he kept her all the same. She had 'soul'. And there were those curls. As the actress Linda Arvidson (Mrs Griffith) put it: 'About her face, so fresh, so pretty, and so gentle, bobbed a dozen or more short golden curls – such perfect little curls as I had never seen.'

Mary Pickford's first film was a one-reeler, *The Violin-Maker of Cremona*, released in June 1909. In this she played opposite the Irish actor, Owen Moore, whom she was to marry (unhappily) two years later. She earned $25 for three days' work, and when agreement was reached for regular work, $25 a week. One of her early films for Griffith which has been preserved, *Simple Charity* (1910) shows precisely what Griffith meant by 'soul'. She plays a maidservant in a tenement with an eye for the handsome doctor who visits an old, destitute couple living in the building; Mary sacrifices her one prized possession, a beautiful dress, to give them money. The action is simple, but Mary brings it a quality of humour, of pathos, of genuine feeling so that you can see everything that passes through her mind. She acts with clarity and discipline, and expresses feelings that everyone can share and understand. She knew her range, and at this stage she stayed well within it; she was therefore completely successful. She was always a lively actress, though with a quiet manner. But underneath the charm and simplicity lay a will of iron, a determination to be successful and to drive a hard bargain for her weekly wages

This determination she inherited from her mother Charlotte, who was of Irish stock from Tralee. Mary had been born a Canadian on 9 April* 1893 in Toronto, and until Belasco had given her the stage name of Mary Pickford (the surname came from her Irish grandfather), she had been plain Gladys Smith, a child actress who had been on the stage with her younger sister Lottie and her brother Jack since the age of five. Charlotte, widowed when she was only 24, was a keen businesswoman who managed her daughter's affairs from this early period of extreme poverty until, through Mary's stardom, they had both become multi-millionaires. The only thing Mary ever kept secret from her mother was her marriage to Owen Moore. The marriage proved an unhappy one – Moore was an alcoholic and Mary, through an accident sustained while filming, was unable ever to have children.

Mary became one of the creators of the star system, and along with Charlie Chaplin its leading exponent. After working on numerous films – mostly comedies – for Griffith at Biograph, she became restless and switched over to a rival company, IMP (Independent Motion Picture Company) where Charlotte was able to improve her daughter's salary from Biograph's $100 to a record $175 a week. Owen, who went with her, caused trouble, and she moved again, finally returning to Biograph. But her name, though known now to the public, still did not appear on the films themselves, and she remained just one of the Biograph girls, along with Blanche Sweet, Mae Marsh, and Lillian and Dorothy Gish. Her best film at this period was *The New York Hat* (1912) written by a 16-year-old girl called Anita Loos and directed by Griffith. She even tried the stage again in her efforts to improve her position.

Her aim was to earn $500 a week before she was 20. She got it (or Charlotte got it for her) from the producer Adolph Zukor (founder of Famous Players, which later became Paramount), and her feature film for him, *Hearts Adrift* (1914) was so successful he agreed to give her $1,000 a week.† She saw herself billed for the first time in lights. She went on then to make the even more successful *Tess of the Storm Country* (1914), for which Zukor coined the publicity slogan, calling her, 'America's sweetheart'. She was to stay with Zukor until 1918 (she settled finally in California in 1917) and during this foundation period for international stardom in American films, she ran neck and neck in star salary ratings with Charlie Chaplin and Douglas Fairbanks, who was to be her future husband, and with whom she fell in love in 1916 when they were both still married to others. The rise in their salaries was phenomenal:

Mary Pickford

1914 $1,000 a week; November $2,000.
1915 $4,000 a week; she is reputed the highest paid woman in the world.
1916 Mutual offer her $1 million a year; Zukor counters with over $1 million, but for two years, with choice of subjects and her own company and studio.
1918 $675,000 for three films (First National), plus $50,000 bonus for Charlotte.
1919 Becomes co-founder of United Artists, and producer of her own films.

* She later changed this to 8 April because this had been her father's birthday!

† Zukor in his book 'The Public is Never Wrong' says without irony of Charlotte that she was 'a very realistic, far-seeing woman' and of Mary, 'I knew her value for the future'.

Charlie Chaplin

1914 $150 to $175 a week (Keystone)
1915 $1,250 a week (Essanay)
1916–17 $10,000 a week, plus $150,000 on signature. (Mutual)
1918–22 $1 million for eight films. (First National)
1919 Co-founder of United Artists.

Douglas Fairbanks

1915 $2,000 a week
1916 $10,000 a week
1919 Co-founder of United Artists.

Mary got the essential thing she needed from Zukor – her name on her films, and eventual choice of subject. Like Chaplin she was exceptionally careful with money, though she appreciated luxury in her home and possession of good clothes and good cars. This was also the period when she established the image which mattered most to her public – the vivacious (if often unfortunate) little girl with the curls, epitomized in *The Poor Little Rich Girl* (1917). Apart from this basic, and eventually recurrent character, she played much else from prostitute to unmarried mother, from a

Below Mary Pickford often played the girl exploited as the result of poverty, as in *The Eternal Grind* (1916).

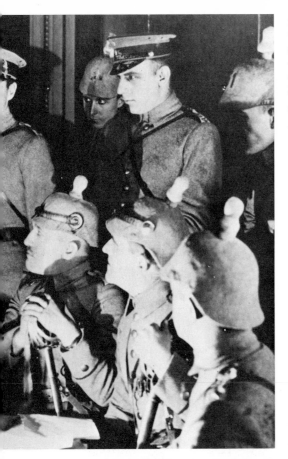

factory worker (*The Eternal Grind*) to a downtrodden Hindu girl (*Less than the Dust*). Many of her films, too, from Griffith onwards, involved social comment on behalf of the oppressed. So great was her acclaim that she toured the country with Fairbanks and Chaplin during the celebrated Liberty Bond drive after America had entered the war in 1917.

Her films for Zukor which had the greatest success were *Rebecca of Sunnybrook Farm* and *Stella Maris* (in which she played a dual role of a workhouse orphan and a wealthy crippled girl). It was a troubled and difficult period for her, however, apart from her success; her developing love-affair with Fairbanks (who was divorced in 1918) was known, and did not exactly match the public's conception of her as the little girl with the curls. She eventually had to buy off her alcoholic husband, and did not get her divorce until 1920, the year she married Douglas on 28 March.* She was 26 and he 36. They spent their honeymoon in Europe; they were mobbed and besieged in every country they visited except Germany, where their films were still unknown.

What was remarkable about Mary Pickford as a star was her restlessness with the child image which brought her the money she and her mother so much desired. She was constantly deviating from it, uneasy because of her

* Mary Pickford had trouble over her divorce and the national scandal it caused, aggravated by the fact that the Attorney-General of the State of Nevada, where she obtained her divorce, subsequently challenged its legality, and consequently that of her marriage to Fairbanks.

Above, left Pickford with her honour at stake at the hands of the Hun in *The Little American* (1917), an anti-German propaganda film.

Left Youth exploited by age: Mary Pickford in *Rebecca of Sunnybrook Farm* (1917).

Pickford and Holbrook Blinn being directed by Ernst Lubitsch for *Rosita* (1923), in which she tried to adopt a sophisticated image.

*Lubitsch and Mary hated each other. But it is only fair to say, as Kevin Brownlow points out in 'The Parade's Gone By', that *Rosita* was hailed as a masterpiece when revived during a Lubitsch festival in Berlin in 1967.

increasing maturity. Zukor wrote of her: 'It is ironical, I suppose, that Mary could not portray on the screen the indomitable woman who was one part of her. . . . The public "typed" Mary against her will. The sweet ingénue with curls was all right, but she wanted to play a variety of roles.' Yet in the films she produced herself she alternated her accepted image (*Daddy Long Legs*, the spirited girl in a hideous orphanage; *Pollyanna*, another ten-year-old orphan) with what were in effect experiments, such as the spectacular *Little Lord Fauntleroy* (in which she played both the fantasy boy-hero and his mother) or her attempts to be sophisticated in *Rosita*, the film she invited Ernst Lubitsch to come from Germany to direct, and which she considered subsequently to be a disaster.* Even when she had reached the age of 32 the public insisted she stay a child; in a

competition launched in 1925 a woman wrote urging her to keep up the illusion of childhood, the illusion 'that you are a little girl in spite of the fact we know you are a grown-up woman'. She remained a kind of Victorian oasis in the swirling eddies of the Jazz Age represented by Gloria Swanson and Clara Bow. So she did her best with *Little Annie Rooney* (1925): 'It was easy for me to act the part of a child because I adored children. I forgot I was grown-up. . . . During a picture I didn't leave the character at the studio, I took it home with me. I lived my parts', she wrote.

Her cameraman, Charles Rosher, worked on virtually all her silent films from 1918 to 1927. Years later, Rosher told Kevin Brownlow: 'On orthochromatic film, hair always looked dark unless you specially lit it. With Mary's curls, lighting was specially important. I often

Left Pickford as the Belgian refugee in *Through the Back Door* (1921).

Mary Pickford in *Pollyanna* (1920). The Pollyanna image – the orphan girl – became the standard one in the eyes of her public. With (extreme left) Helen Jerome Eddy, Doc Crane (centre) and Herbert Prior (second from right).

arranged her curls myself; I kept the hairpins by the camera. I also selected her make-up, which she applied herself.'

Mary became, in effect, the Queen of Holly-wood during the 1920s. Pickfair, the mansion in Beverly Hills which Douglas had built, and which he gave her, became the centre to which crowned heads, dukes, and the famous of the world were drawn, yet neither she nor Douglas were able to give it the quality of a *salon* they so much desired. It remained curiously old-fashioned, even dull, in spite of their lavish hospitality. Mary's single rivals at the time were Gloria Swanson (the only other woman star at the time who produced her own films) and Marion Davies, by virtue of being the fabulous newspaper proprietor Hearst's mistress and helping him entertain in San Simeon, California's most extravagant mansion. But

the great parties given at Pickfair became celebrated. Only towards the end did things begin to go wrong. Charlotte, who controlled Mary's life, died in 1928, the year Mary officially had her curls cut off in the presence of the press.* Her marriage – a true one – entered on a difficult period leading to a divorce in 1936 because of Douglas's unfortunate infatuation with Sylvia Ashley. Mary subsequently married the devoted Charles 'Buddy' Rogers who joined her in Pickfair. Douglas married Sylvia Ashley, but there seems little doubt he and Mary should never have broken their marriage; she was profoundly distressed when he died in 1939, the same year as Owen Moore. Douglas was given a posthumous Academy Award in the same year for his unique contribution to the international development of the film. He had been the Academy's first President on its

* Six of these celebrated curls are preserved – 'two in a museum-case at Pickfair, and two each at museums in San Diego and Los Angeles' (Robert Windeler in 'Sweetheart').

Opposite page Clara Bow as a cover girl on an early film magazine.

Right Pathos and charm in *Little Annie Rooney* (1925), in which, in her thirties, Mary Pickford tried to maintain her child image.

The only time Mary Pickford appeared with her husband Douglas Fairbanks on the screen was in *The Taming of the Shrew* (1929), the first sound film version of a Shakespeare play to be produced.

* This is indeed what the Biograph executives had told Griffith in 1909, ordering him to sack her. He argued them out of it. See 'The Man who Invented Hollywood: the Autobiography of D. W. Griffith', p. 78.

foundation twelve years earlier in 1927.

It is ironic that Mary won her Oscar from the newly founded Academy for her utterly untypical performance in a melodrama called *Coquette* (1929). 'I am sick of Cinderella parts', she had said. 'I want to wear smart clothes and play the lover.' She played the Southern vamp, short skirts, illicit love and all, with a tragic outcome alike for the boy involved and her father. It was a sound film and her voice, though high pitched, proved adequate. Then in the midst of a breaking marriage, she had for the only time played opposite Douglas in the over-maligned version of *The Taming of the Shrew*; the play is after all Shakespearean slapstick, and that is how they played it, with

much wordless pantomime. Referring to *The Taming of the Shrew*, Mary herself said, 'The making of that film was my finish. My confidence was completely shattered, and I was never again at ease before the camera or microphone.' She quarrelled with Rosher, her faithful cameraman for 12 years, and blamed the director, Sam Taylor, for failures, real or imagined, though he later directed her last, pathetic effort at sophistication, *Kiki* (1931), in which she played a French chorus-girl. Her final film, the sentimental *Secrets* (1933, directed by Frank Borzage, and co-starring a youthful Leslie Howard) told the story of a marriage from youth to age. In order to reinforce her sophistication she played in 'Coquette' on the stage during the 1930s, but in effect her career was finished, though she was only 37. So she retired, taking greatly to spiritualism, a little to alcohol, and continually to tough business negotiation in the affairs and disputes of United Artists, from which she only sold out in 1953. In 1934 she published a book, 'Why not try God?', and in 1955 her tape-recorded, lightly sketched autobiography, 'Sunshine and Shadow'.

In 'Sunshine and Shadow' Mary tells the story of how she and Charlie Chaplin once stood together in front of a mirror. Charlie (who in his heart always wanted to be tall and handsome, instead of short and mercurial) complained his head was too big for his slight body and his arms too short. 'What about me?' said Mary. 'My head is too big for my body and my arms are too long for it.* And I'm a woman, Charlie.'

Theda Bara

Theda Bara belonged to the period when the producer made the star and, subsequently, the star the producer. Both in name and conception as a screen image she was a special creation. She was, first of all, the product of William Fox and his assistant, Winfield Sheehan, who were responsible for the Fox Film Company (established 1914), which was much later (1935) to merge with Twentieth Century to make the well-known company of Twentieth Century-Fox. Fox, a former vaudeville performer born in Hungary, had become a successful showman turned film-producer.

The fortunes of Fox were founded on their well-calculated investment in this rather special kind of lady – a small-time stage actress, Theodosia Goodman, born 1890 in Cincinnati, Ohio. Her prime interest appears to have been twofold – spiritualism, and creating an exotic image for herself as a teenager on the New York stage, using her mother's name, de Coppet, and dyeing her hair black. She used the dark-ringed eye make-up fashionable at the period and liked to affect a highly artificial foreign accent. Her introduction to the Fox studios came through their director, Frank Powell, who thought her sufficiently talented in this artificial kind of charade to warrant the risk of casting her for Fox's 1915 production of *A Fool There Was*.*

Theodosia, aged now 25, was more attracted by the salary ($150 a week) than the part for which she was cast, but the studio had their hold on her and set about moulding her into what was to become one of the screen's most memorably exotic and primitive stars. But first of all they had to make a new name for her – Theda (from Theodosia) and Bara (from her Swiss grandfather's middle name – Barranger). At the same time their publicists put out the notorious legend that the names were anagrams respectively for Death and Arab because her father was an Italian artist and her mother an Arab princess, and that she had enjoyed an exotic career in the French theatre before coming to the United States. Theda Bara became her legal name in 1917.

A Fool There Was concerned the absolute ruin to which a vampire-woman brought a distinguished diplomat – the *femme fatale* who reduces her man to a drivelling 'fool'. 'Kiss me, my fool,' she says over his spent body. The total opposite of Mary Pickford, the wholesome, affectionate, mischievous tomboy, this woman stood for evil incarnate; she sucked the soul of a man as the price of sex. The film proved phenomenally successful. The publicity photographs which were put out to sustain the image in the film pictured her as a dark-eyed siren with a sensual mouth and heavy lidded eyes covered in kohl. She was swathed in lengths of cloth which left her arms and shoulders bare while she posed in brooding triumph over the prone skeletons of her victims.

Bara's career of symbolic female vice was now assured. For the public the films in which she appeared in quick succession had a two-way attraction: they fed their audience's suppressed appetite for sin and at the same time bolstered their consciences by turning these excitingly melodramatic fables into virtuous tracts. The wages of sin were death and self-destruction; all her films were highly moral parables of retribution. Bara made 39 films in four years – almost a film a month – a considerable feat even taking into account the remarkable turn-over possible in silent film-making. She created a legend second only to that of Pickford, all the more successful because there was no possibility of confusing the two. Her heavy mouth, broad nostrils, dark hair and staring, black-rimmed eyes loomed from the screen and from publicity photographs in a ceaseless, inescapable flow. She was everyone's idea of the Satanic female. It became her mask, and she was to become as trapped in its image as Pickford was in hers.

Theodosia in private life was a simple, surburban woman with her faith pinned to spiritualism. Yet she had, for publicity's sake, to make out that playing the vampire-woman called up hidden responses in her soul. At a celebrated press conference held in the Blackstone Hotel in Chicago she gave her interview swathed in furs in a room made suffocatingly hot to match (it was said) her over-heated

Opposite page Theda Bara as Salome (1918), a role played by many of the screen's 'love goddesses'.

* The title comes from Kipling's poem inspired by Burne-Jones's picture of a macabre woman, 'The Vampire'. The poem, with the same title, runs:

A fool there was and he made his prayer
(Even as you and I!)
To a rag and a bone and a hank of hair
(We called her the woman who did not care)
But the fool he called her his lady fair –
(Even as you and I!)

The poem had inspired both a novel and a play with the title, 'A Fool There Was', and their popularity had inspired the film.

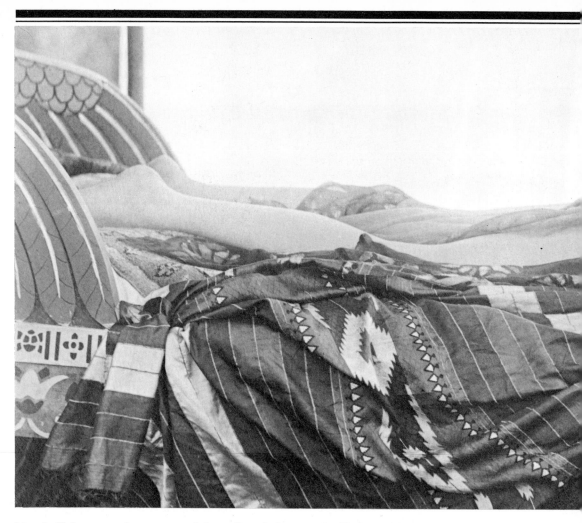

Theda Bara did not confine her vamps to the contemporary scene. She drew on the classic 'love goddesses', including *Cleopatra* (1917).

blood. 'I have made an especial study of the type,' she told the press. 'I hope I have succeeded in depicting the complex emotions of the panther woman as vividly as they have appealed to me.'

She played a husband-stealer in *The Kreutzer Sonata* (adapted from Tolstoy), a woman who leads a man to destroy his wife in *The Clemenceau Case*, a lustful gipsy in *Carmen*, a mass-destroyer in *Destruction*, an evil force in *Gold and the Woman* and *The Eternal Sappho*, and 'the champion vampire of the season' in *The Tiger Woman*. In vain she pleaded for more sympathetic roles, and Fox yielded from time to time – she played an orphan in a story of the French Revolution, *The Two Orphans*, and (remarkably) Juliet in *Romeo and Juliet*, for which her lips were narrowed, losing some of their assumed sensuality. In *Heart and Soul* she was permitted to sacrifice her life for her lover. Her urge to play noted stage roles led to her appearing in *Camille* as the doomed courtesan and in *Cleopatra* as history's most celebrated siren, a film which was again an outstanding success. She was in turn Salome mad with desire for Herod and in *The Light* the wickedest woman in Paris. She even began to write her own material, and produced in *The Soul of Buddha* the part of a priestess who desecrates her temple through sinful love.

What is interesting about Theda Bara is the ambivalent attitude she adopted to playing the vamp. In a sense she anticipated her own self-destruction as an actress, for the part she embodied could not survive the teens of the century in the exaggerated form which had made her famous in 1915. As early as 1919 she said, 'Always I have been a charlatan, a register of human emotions. It may be because all intense feeling is pretence. . . . Today I regret the profligacy of my emotions.' She had continued, however, to fulfil public demand for the vamp as long as it lasted, and indeed somewhat beyond, because she was trapped in it. The public did not want to see her as anything else, preferring simply to tire of her and forget her. She tried in 1919 to play the Irish colleen in *Kathleen Mavourneen*; the cinema was picketed by the Irish objecting to a Jewish vamp impersonating a pure Irish girl. In any case, the film was a disaster at the box-office. But Fox insisted she play the vamp to the last drop of blood (her own, as well as that of her victims) and then, as this out-of-date image faded, he refused to renew her contract which had risen by then to $4,000 a week. She wanted $5,000, but she was no longer worth a small fraction of it.

Theda Bara was never to succeed again on the screen, or for that matter on the stage, where she tried come-backs at various times right into the 1930s. Alexander Woollcott wrote of her stage appearances in 1920 in a melodrama, 'The Blue Flame', 'She is pretty bad, but not bad enough to be remembered always.' It was a play involving the supernatural, but the Broadway audience laughed at her. In 1921 she married her film-director, Charles J. Brabin,

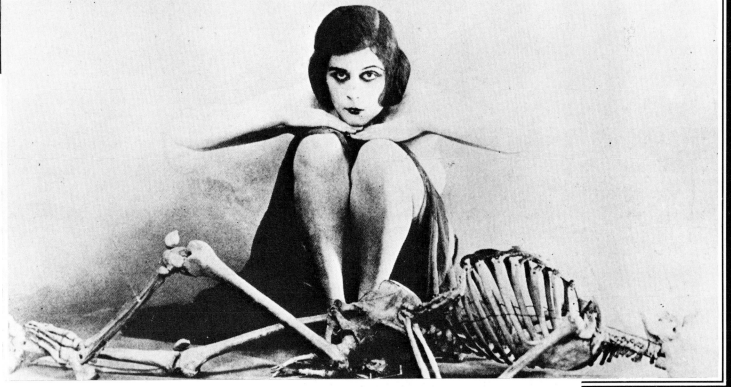

Below A publicity still for Theda Bara at the beginning of her career as the star man-eater in *A Fool There Was* (1914).

who was born in England and eventually gave her an English accent; his professional success enabled her to become a Hollywood hostess.

Looking back on her career in 1950, she herself said, 'To understand those days, you must consider that people believed what they saw on the screen. . . . They thought that the stars of the screen were the way they saw them. Now they know it is all make-believe.'

It should be remembered that Theda Bara was a beautiful woman underneath the concealing make-up. In some of her later films (which do not survive) one can see this from the stills in which her face is relatively free from the mask of disguise – such as *La Belle Russe* (1919), or one of her later attempts at a comeback, *The Unchastened Woman* (1925). But her vamp was a humourless spectacle, lacking even sexual vitality, and her acting talent was insufficient to enable her to succeed outside the limited range in which she had enjoyed such unprecedented (but limited) success.

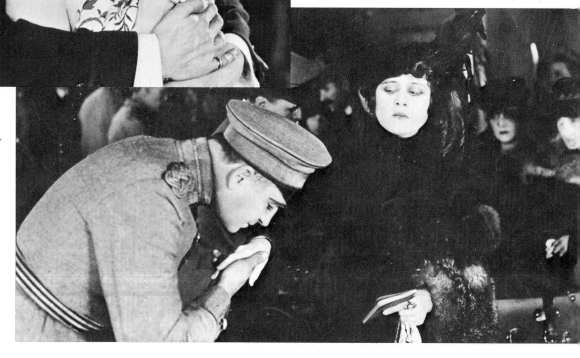

Right and opposite As Poppaea, a nurse who becomes a 'modern vampire', but is later purified by her love for a young student in *When A Woman Sins* (1918). This film was publicized as 'the greatest woman's story ever told'.

Above Bara as the wife, neglected by her husband Windham Standing in *The Unchastened Woman* (1925), strives to win him back through jealousy.

Right Theda Bara in *When Men Desire* (1919) exploited the theme of the exotic, predatory woman.

THE NINETEEN TWENTIES

The 1920s is really the beginning of the modern period – the real 20th century. The First World War precipitated the great changes of our time – the foundation of the Soviet Union, the Fascist build-up more particularly in Italy and Germany which led to the Second World War, the demolition of the British Empire, and the ascendancy of the United States as the primary power in the world in direct rivalry with the Soviet Union. These big political and social changes were accompanied, less spectacularly, by the erosion of the strictures of the old-time class system and the dominance of traditional bourgeois morality. On the intellectual and cultural level, the 1920s saw the popularization of the new psychology associated originally with Freud, the decline in the influence of conventional religion, the open interest in sex and a freer way of life among young people, the liberating writings of Shaw, Wells and the earlier D.H. Lawrence, and the de-conventionalizing of art into the more esoteric, disintegrating forms of Cubism, Dada, and Surrealism.

On the more popular level, this new outlook found expression most quickly in the United States, which as a nation relishes anything new and revels in the sensational. Unlike Britain, the American film industry did not yet have any formal kind of film censorship, and certain of the more enterprising producers were, therefore, ready to run the gauntlet of the moral pressure groups in the States (who were very strong and vocal) by producing 'daring' films. In the van was Cecil B. De Mille, with such films as *Male and Female* (1919) and *Why Change your Wife?* (1920). He was closely followed by Erich von Stroheim with his European sophistication; Stroheim successfully challenged the box-office with his films which set America agog to learn about the wicked 'continental' ways across the Atlantic. For America, too, it was the Jazz Age. Films were to be made with sensational titles like, *Poisoned Paradise*, *The Primrose Path*, *Dangerous Curves*, *Dancing Mothers*, and *It*.

Correspondingly, actresses had to come out of their shells and live it up on the screen. The old-fashioned, 'Pollyanna' image represented by Mary Pickford was definitely out; even she had had to bend a little before the winds of change and (as we have seen) she invited another sophisticate from Europe, Ernst Lubitsch, to direct a film for her – *Rosita* (1923). Though this was not a success, Lubitsch was the following year to make a personal reputation in America with *Forbidden Paradise* and *The Marriage Circle*.

But the actresses of the 1920s were, in their period style, sex if not exactly love goddesses. By the later 1920s the sophisticated image took over, adopting its own strange forms – bobbed hair, short (above the knee) skirts, and a thin, Twiggy-like figure with a flat, compressed 'chest'. There were the dangerous 'flappers' of Constance Bennett as in *Code of the West*, or the husband-stealer in *My Wife and I*; there were *risqué* subjects for Bebe Daniels – *Singed Wings*, *Unguarded Women*, *Sinners in Heaven*, *Miss Bluebeard* – a creature garbed in feathers and lace.

Girls in the swim tended to abandon the languorous and sensual for the hectic and frenetic. They drank and smoked like the boys; they danced the Charleston through the night, they outdid the men in sport, in driving fast cars, living it up with men like sexy tomboys. Their mothers, brought up on Mary Pickford, were duly horrified. But even they read the fashionable best-sellers by Elinor Glyn, the exotic British novelist whose scandalous novel, 'Three Weeks' was filmed in Hollywood and set the pace in 1924.

Elinor Glyn was the doyenne of drawing-room sex; she referred to attractiveness and sexiness as 'It', and girls who had this quality as 'It' girls. Elinor Glyn became the middle-aged socialite leader in Hollywood – she had the exact measure of her public and of the industry, which was both excited by subjects that turned on sex and alarmed at the militant attitude of the moralists who were doing their best to have 'advanced' films banned, State by State, and to banish from the screen those whose private lives created scandal, which included Fatty Arbuckle (involved in a horrifying case of a girl's death due to a cruel form of sexual assault), Mabel Normand, and (though he managed to survive through sheer popularity) Charlie Chaplin, who was involved during the period in two divorces made notorious by the press. Even Mary Pickford and Douglas Fairbanks had had their troubles, having to get divorced in 1920 in order to marry, only to be in trouble again at the end of the decade and finally divorced from each other in 1936. Hollywood's name was blackened by many smears and rumours, and Will H. Hays was appointed in 1922 to establish controls over the industry through the Motion Picture

Left Marion Davies in *The Cardboard Lover* (1928). A spirited actress, she owed her stardom to the backing she received from William Randolph Hearst, the press magnate.

Below Mary Astor in *The Sunset Derby* (1927). A girl of character, she complained at this period that she was condemned by the studios to play 'the insipid *ingénue*'.

Producers and Distributors Association of America, though the celebrated Censorship Code was not established until 1930, backed in 1934 by the establishment of the most formidable of outside pressure groups, the Legion of Decency, which had the full support of the Catholic church.

The girl who embodied 'It' during the silent period was Clara Bow. While the image of innocence was maintained not only by Mary Pickford but by a few other stars such as Lillian Gish and Janet Gaynor, the age of sophistication was represented not only by Clara Bow, Constance Bennett, Mabel Normand and Bebe Daniels but by other leading actresses of the 1920s, including Pola Negri, Greta Garbo, and Vilma Banky from Europe, and from America, Mae Murray, Myrna Loy, Norma and Constance Talmadge, Marion Davies, Colleen Moore, Dolores Costello, Mary Astor, and Betty Compson. It was a formidable regiment of women who flaunted their antic vitality from the screens of the world, America's most highly visible export.

Clara Bow

Clara Bow was only to be an 'It' girl in a fraction of her films – she too tried many other kinds of image, but the 'It' girl she remains, symbol of the Jazz Age. As a star she was made by her appearance in the film *It* (1927) for Paramount, based on Elinor Glyn's novel. She had reached the screen by one of the hallowed routes – success in a beauty contest, bit parts in films during the early 1920s, then contract player in star roles from 1926 for Paramount. The bit parts included an appearance in the smart Lubitsch picture, *Kiss Me Again* in 1925, the same year she established herself as a 'flapper' type in *The Plastic Age*.

For Paramount she starred as a fully emancipated flapper (1920s version) in *Dancing Mothers* (1926). This was her box-office image, the thing she did really well. She was not an actress of great versatility, but she had 'It' – which meant limitless energy and bounce, and the kind of vibrantly feminine good looks which came to be called 'cute'. Her hair was bobbed and short, her lips pursed together under a neatly painted Cupid's bow, and her brown eyes were lively, sparkling, and turned knowingly towards men. Her fashionable contemporary, Anita Loos, the scriptwriter and novelist, author of 'Gentlemen prefer Blondes', said that she managed to be at once 'innocuous and flashy'. Although you could not see it, her hair was fiery red. She was every girl's idea of what a girl should be in an age of immature emancipation, short skirts, cigarette-holders, jazz, and such bootleg alcohol as could be come by. The height of her fame was reached in the era just before sound, the middle years of the 1920s, yet, like Pickford, she became imprisoned in her own self-made mould, and the studio felt she must stay in it even when the image was quickly dying in the dawn of a new era, the 1930s. By the age of 26 she had retired.

She was born in 1905 in Brooklyn, New York – her father was an odd-job man, her mother a permanent invalid. Like Chaplin, she experienced extreme poverty and the sadness of having a mother who was mentally unstable. When in 1921 Clara won the 'Fame and Fortune' contest sponsored by a film fan magazine group, her mother threatened her with a knife; she had to be committed to a mental home and she died in 1923. From this period until 1925, the year of *The Plastic Age*, Clara appeared with some success in over 20 films, her status gradually improving, especially when she was put under contract by a small-time independent producer, B.P. Schulberg, who was later to take her to Paramount, which he rejoined as a producer in 1925 after his own independent company had failed. Schulberg, at first doubtful of her, had given her a rigorous screen test without benefit of make-up or any advance preparation, pressing her at speed through the emotional range he considered necessary for an actress – 'Laugh,' he ordered; then suddenly, 'Stop. Now Cry.' The laughter died immediately, and she cried, the tears pouring down her cheeks. She was in.

During this initial period of her career, before she joined Paramount, she appeared in a variety of parts: for example, during 1924 in *Grit* (script by F. Scott Fitzgerald) she was a refugee from a reformatory, in *Black Oxen* a flapper in love with an older man, in *Poisoned Paradise* (that is, Monte Carlo) an amateur gambler out to break the bank, in *Wine* (according to 'Variety') 'a giddy young thing'. But the flapper image appeared again in 1925 in *Eve's Lover*, though in Lubitsch's comedy, *Kiss Me Again*, and in *The Primrose Path*, in which she was a night-club artiste, she was more sophisticatedly wicked. The flapper finally won, with Clara's special qualities of real, quite endearing vitality, in *The Plastic Age*, in which she played a co-ed in a story exposing the evils of studies abandoned for jazz and high living. James Robert Parrish describes her as, 'part of the collegiate fast set in which rolled stockings, cigarettes, bootleg booze, Charleston dancing, snappy talk, and petting were everything'. According to 'The New York Times', 'she knows how to use lips, shoulders and all the rest of her tiny self in the most effective manner. She radiates an elfin sensuousness.'

It was this film that finally enabled Schulberg to put her under contract to Paramount, though she appeared in several more indifferent films before she became Paramount's 'property'. By now her contract with Schulberg as an independent was considered to be worth $25,000, the sum Paramount paid him for her 'take-over'. Her first film for them was *Dancing Mothers* (1926), in which she played the daughter of the star (Alice Joyce), and under Herbert Brenon's direction, according to 'Variety', abandoned any attempt to act she may have tried in the past, deciding to 'just be herself'. She was even more successful in *Mantrap* (director, Victor Fleming), in which she was the incorrigibly flirtatious young wife of an elderly husband. In *Kid Boots* (1926) she appeared with Eddie Cantor (his first film).

Then she played in the film with which she was to become identified, adapted from Elinor Glyn's novel, 'It'. What is 'It'? Elinor Glyn had her own description, and made a personal appearance in the film as a celebrity in order to expound it: 'To have "It", the fortunate possessor must have that strange magnetism which attracts both sexes. "It" is a purely virile quality, belonging to a strong character. He or she must be entirely unself-conscious and full of self-confidence, indifferent to the effect he or she is producing, and uninfluenced by others. There must be physical attraction, but beauty is unnecessary. Conceit or self-consciousness destroys "It" immediately.' But when asked by a reporter to tell him what 'It' was, all Clara could say was, 'I ain't real sure.' That, I suppose, is one reason why she had 'It'.

'It' is, therefore, more than sex-appeal,

though this is an important ingredient. It is a natural, unassumed vitality, only too easy to destroy by any kind of self-conscious sophistication. Clara Bow genuinely had this natural, feminine vitality, her directly flirtatious response to men being without guile or pretension. In 'It' she played a salesgirl who falls in love with the rich owner of the store in which she works, and she plays her hand so well she wins his love. Like Pickford, she set a hairstyle for a generation, although of a totally different pattern. Girls by the million tried to look like Clara Bow. Zukor, head of Paramount, wrote of her, 'Clara Bow had served, with reason, as Elinor Glyn's model for the "It" personality. Clara was exactly the same off the screen as on. She danced even when her feet were not moving. Some part of her was in motion in all her waking moments – if only her great rolling eyes. Though not beautiful, Clara was a striking girl, with red hair, a soft, heart-shaped face, and a plump figure. Yet it was an elemental magnetism – sometimes described as animal vitality – that made her the centre of attraction in any company.'

The problem was to keep 'It' a going concern. In 1927 – the year her salary reached $2,700 a week, and her weekly fan mail totalled 40,000 letters – she was to be seen in various kinds of story – as the seductive little Red Cross nurse (she was only 5 foot 3½ inches in height) in Wellman's *Wings*, in which she is in love with Buddy Rogers, who plays an Air Service pilot, as a spoilt rich girl after a married man in Victor Fleming's *Hula* (which had censorship trouble), and as a vamp in Dorothy Arzner's *Get Your Man*. In *Children of Divorce* (with Gary Cooper) she commits suicide as a result of too much sex.

In her private life she lived pretty freely, preferring always informal dress, games of poker, quick love-affairs and no ties or conventions. Harry Richman, a night-club singer, attracted her. She was briefly engaged; he called her, 'the sexiest woman I ever saw'. She was never a Hollywood socialite; she preferred dives to dinner-parties. Her behaviour remained rough and her language fruity. She loved gambling, often for high stakes. Her brief love-affairs (with Gary Cooper, or with Victor Fleming, for example) often drove her close to nervous collapse. In *Red Hair* (1928) a sequence in early Technicolor showed her red hair to advantage when she posed in a white bathing-suit, and she frequently appeared in costumes or underclothes which showed off her 'ripe' figure. At the height of her fame she would ride in an open car with seven red Chow dogs chosen to match her hair. In *The Wild Party* (1929) she talked for the first time in the part of a college student who makes her professor (Fredric March) fall for her and call her his

Above Clara Bow with Antonio Moreno in *It* (1927), the most famous image-making role, derived from Elinor Glyn's notorious 'sex' novel.

Right Bow with Clive Brook in *Hula* (1927), which gave her the chance to dominate her man.

'little savage'. Her voice was passable ('quite good', says Zukor) but it was unsophisticated, 'low class' and nasal. She sang contralto in *Paramount on Parade* (1930). But, according to Zukor, her inability to stand still told against getting satisfactory recordings of her dialogue during the early, restrictive days of sound equipment.

So the films continued to pour out – such as *Dangerous Curves* (1929, about circus life), and *Love among the Millionaires* (1930) – and by now her salary had risen to $5,000 a week. But her wildness finally caught up with her in unpleasant court cases; in 1930 she was involved (through error of judgment) in vast gambling debts at blackjack (pontoon) in Nevada, while in 1931 she sued her former secretary for misuse of an open cheque and for blackmail. Lurid stories of her way of life came to light; her public was alienated, and the film that followed did no business. As a result she suffered a nervous relapse, and she had to be replaced by other stars in films in which she should have featured. She quarrelled with Paramount, either because she wanted to retire before her contract had expired or because they wanted to be rid of her. 'A sex symbol is always a heavy load to carry, especially when one is very tired, hurt and

Above Bow in William Wellman's *Wings* (1927), in which she appeared rather irrelevantly as 'sex-interest'.

Left Clara Bow with Gilbert Roland and Donald Keith in *The Plastic Age* (1925), which condemned the effect of jazz and sex on the young.

Above Clara Bow as a half-caste in *Call Her Savage* (1932).

Right Clara Bow as the gold-digger who reformed in time to close *Red Hair* (1928). This film exploited her beautiful colouring.

bewildered,' she said.

In 1931, at the age of 24, she suddenly married the cowboy star, Rex Bell, a wealthy actor with a vast ranch in Nevada. Eventually, after many rumours, she returned to the screen with renewed vitality in 1932 in a melodrama, *Call her Savage*, and appeared as a hula-dancer in *Hoopla* (1933). Her contract was worth $125,000 a picture. But more to the point were the two sons she had by Bell in 1934 and 1938, while Bell became Lieutenant-Governor of Nevada in 1954. Her mental disturbances returned, however, and she took to living in sanatoria in Los Angeles and elsewhere; she became a recluse, separated from her husband. In 1960 she issued the celebrated statement, 'I slip my old crown of "It" girl not to Taylor or Bardot, but to Monroe.' When her husband died in 1962, in spite of the separation she emerged to attend his funeral. But her mind finally gave way completely, and she died in her home, a bungalow in Culver City, in September 1965.

Gloria Swanson

Gloria Swanson, with Mary Pickford, was among the first great professional stars. Her date of birth is said to be 1898, and she was born in Chicago; her father, being a civilian worker for the Army, moved his family from place to place. After working as a clerk, Gloria took to appearing as an extra in films at the Essanay studios in Chicago. Her ambition was to be a dramatic actress, so Essanay (where she was tested by Chaplin) was scarcely the right studio for her. Nevertheless, she worked with Wallace Beery in a series of comedies in 1916 and married him the same year; the marriage broke up three years later, when both of them went to Hollywood. Here she began work for Mack Sennett at his Keystone studios for (according to Zukor, who later employed her) $65 a week, and stayed with him until 1918.

Her approach to comedy was unusual: 'I was funny,' she said, looking back to this period, 'because I didn't try to be funny. The more serious I got, the funnier the scene became.' But the spirit of independence was already strong in her at the age of 20, and she left Sennett because, as she thought, he was trying to make her into a copy of Mabel Normand, his over-favoured actress. 'I told him I didn't want to be a second anybody, so he tore up my

contract,' Gloria claims. She went to Triangle, and starred in eight dramatic pictures in 1918 with titles such as *Society for Sale*, *Everywoman's Husband* and *Wife or Country*.

It was then that she had her break. She went to work for Cecil B. De Mille at Paramount. With him she came to represent the height of sophistication known at this period, offering a strong foretaste of the style of the 1920s. The films in which De Mille starred her were in fact moral parables in which the wages of sin are clearly spelt out in the finale after actress and audience have enjoyed their self-indulgence to the full during the earlier phases of the film. The titles were deliberately provocative – *Don't Change Your Husband* (1919), in which a bored woman leaves a staid husband only to marry another man who is unfaithful, *For Better for Worse* (1919), *Why Change your Wife?* (1920), in which she succeeds in outglamourizing the rival for her husband's affections and, above all, *Male and Female* (1919), adapted from Barrie's play, 'The Admirable Crichton', in which she plays the society girl who appropriates the highly practical family butler, Crichton (Thomas Meighan), when he and the family who employ him are wrecked on a desert island.

There is no doubt that these and the other films she made for De Mille set the pace for the 1920s; glamour and seduction went hand in hand with inevitable retribution, but not before the audience had received a heady vision of Swanson's sexual exhibitionism. 'Make it sleeveless, backless, skirtless – in short, go to the limit,' she cries to her costumier in *Why Change your Wife?*. To universalize her female splendour, De Mille anticipated his later Biblical spectacles by putting symbolic insets into *Don't Change Your Husband*, in which Swanson is seen as the Goddess of Love and Pleasure, and into *Male and Female*, which includes a Babylonian episode showing her as a sex-slave to Meighan's imperial lord. However, the moral message in these films certainly backfires, as Alexander Walker has perspicaciously pointed out: 'The remedy that De Mille often suggests is a reshuffle of marriage partners. . . . The best way to stay happily married is to act as if one is not married at all.' He regards De Mille's and Swanson's films as in part responsible for the breakdown in moral values in America of the 1920s.

De Mille, with Swanson as his model, was more responsible than anyone for making Hollywood films the vehicle for exaggerated *haute couture*, for extravagant grooming and hair-styling, and for luxurious interior decoration. Swanson's elegant body was seen swathed in the most extraordinary garbs, which flowed down into trains around her feet, or she appeared in stages of undress calculated to excite her more sex-starved audiences.

Swanson also completed a series of films for Sam Wood; the titles alone are enough to reveal their nature and show the erotic glamour they suggested – *Under the Lash*, *Don't Tell Everything*, *Beyond the Rocks* (1922, with Valentino),

Gloria Swanson plays an unhappy wife whom Rudolph Valentino charms in *Beyond The Rocks* (1922).

Her Gilded Cage, My American Wife (1923, with Antonio Moreno), *Prodigal Daughters*, and *Bluebeard's Eighth Wife* (the silent version). By now she was a top star, earning $20,000 a week in the early 1920s, the undoubted rival in public estimation of Mary Pickford, whom she was upstaging and outdating, or Pola Negri, the star Paramount had brought from Europe in 1923 well before either Garbo or Dietrich, representing European as distinct from the native, American brand of 1920s screen sophistication, such as Colleen Moore. Moore and Negri earned at this period some $7,000 a week. 'She was no great beauty,' writes Zukor of Swanson, 'but her face, with big, silver-blue eyes and wide mouth with even teeth, photographed well. . . . She developed into a com-

petent actress.' She was very short, only 5 foot 2 inches.

When Paramount had to tie her with a new contract in 1923, she drove as hard a bargain as the Pickfords could ever have done, and insisted on having a full say in the choice of her subjects. Hundreds of thousands of dollars were expended on her gowns and costumes, an expense fully publicized to the world at large. People were led to believe she never wore the same gown twice. She was known in the fan magazines as 'Queen of the Movies'. Star status was a position she both understood and peremptorily demanded, 'I have decided that when I am a star I will be every inch and every moment a star,' she declared, and this, like other of her professional declarations, has been

Left Gloria Swanson in *For Better For Worse* (1919). The subject is a contemporary woman's discovery of her lover's courage, which she had doubted. De Mille inserted flashbacks into the past in order to emphasize his theme with parallel stories.

Swanson in another of her unhappy wife roles in *A Society Scandal* (1924).

quoted ever since. 'In those days they wanted us to live like kings. So we did, and why not?'

On the set, according to Zukor, she could be temperamental. Her natural successor, as Alexander Walker has pointed out, is Elizabeth Taylor, a 'love goddess' if ever there was one, whose life style is conceived in terms of a shop-girl's delirium. The dream was crowned when, after making *Zaza, The Humming Bird, A Society Scandal, Manhandled* and *The Wages of Virtue*, she went to France to star in *Madame Sans-Gêne* in 1925 – Zukor says, to separate her from her dire rival in the studio, Pola Negri. She returned with the Marquis de la Falaise de la Coudraye as her new (and third) husband.* The French were so excited by her presence that they decorated her with the Legion of Honour; in Hollywood she was welcomed back at the première of *Madame Sans-Gêne* by the audience singing 'Home, Sweet Home'.

The films that she was making were nothing but vehicles for her stardom, and she was dissatisfied. There was one remaining ambition to be fulfilled – to equal Mary Pickford and become her own producer. Turning down the $18,000 a week that Paramount was prepared to give to keep her, she became her own producer by joining the consortium of talent at United

* She had meanwhile been married briefly to a businessman named Sombron.

Opposite page Sadie Thompson (1928) starred Gloria Swanson in the title role of a film based on Somerset Maugham's story 'Rain'.

Right Gloria Swanson and Lionel Barrymore in *Sadie Thompson* (1928). Her interpretation of Maugham's archetypal whore won her an Academy nomination in the first year of Oscars.

Below Swanson in *The Trespasser* (1929). The subject of her first sound film was mother-love.

Artists. Now, at the age of 28, she was able to present herself in subjects of her own selection. *The Loves of Sunya* (1927), her first, was scarcely successful. But with *Queen Kelly* (1928; co-produced by her in association with Joseph Kennedy, father of the future President), she met with disaster. Aiming high, she chose Erich von Stroheim, the most sophisticated, talented, and most extravagant of the directors originating from central Europe, to direct her in this story of an orphaned schoolgirl stolen by a prince from a convent and subjected to the raging jealousy of his fiancée, the Queen. Stroheim not only wrote the story and screenplay, but shared in the art direction. He ran her deeply into debt before the film was finished and, although completed by Edmund Goulding with a special ending – the girl's suicide – created by Swanson for Europe, the film was never to be screened in the States.

Swanson recouped some, but not all of her losses with *Sadie Thompson* (from Somerset Maugham's 'Rain') and *The Trespasser* (1929), her first sound film. But, though her voice was more than adequate, her screen image had begun to date, and her final run-down of films (all comedies) from *What a Widow!* (1930) to *Perfect Understanding* (1933, with Laurence Olivier) ended her great, if brief career at the height of stardom. Apart from spasmodic appearances in the theatre and occasionally in indifferent films, she did nothing of importance

GLORIA SWANSON
in
"Sadie Thompson"

Based on the Story by W. SOMERSET MAUGHAM
Directed by RAOUL WALSH

- UNITED ARTISTS PICTURE -

36

until her sensational return to Paramount as Norma Desmond, star of Billy Wilder's *Sunset Boulevard* (1950), which was to be by far her most memorable part.

Norma Desmond is an heroic monument to the monomania of stardom in the silent period. Its satire is effective because it is so deeply felt by an actress who understood exactly what she was satirizing and had herself lived the same dream. But the film was scarcely understood by the mass audiences of 1950, and was a critical but not a commercial success. Though ever since it has made the name of Gloria Swanson renowned in film history, it did not lead to a revival in her career. Since then she has played in occasional, and poor-quality films. But her courage – and it needed courage to accept such a part in *Sunset Boulevard*, in which both De Mille and Stroheim themselves appeared – was marked, and in 1974, well in her seventies, she was working on *Airport '75*, dressed by the veteran Hollywood *couturière*, Edith Head, who had designed her clothes for *Sunset Boulevard*, and has dressed so many great stars from Marlene Dietrich and Mae West to Elizabeth Taylor.

THE NINETEEN THIRTIES

Opposite, above In *The Thin Man* (1934) and successive films which originated from Dashiell Hammett's story, Myrna Loy appeared as the sophisticated girl, one of the team of the private eye and his wife which set a new convention for the comedy thriller.

Opposite, below As Charles Laughton's bride sent by mail order in Kanin's unusual love story, *They Knew What They Wanted* (1940), Carole Lombard brought individuality to her performance.

The great divide between the 1920s and the 1930s was first of all the arrival of sound, spread over the period 1928 to 1930. Many stars failed to survive the transition, making the 1930s a new era for stars if not for directors, most of whom survived by learning the new techniques of movies with sound. One of the great acquisitions, however, was George Cukor, who came to Hollywood as a dialogue director and was to become celebrated for his sensitive direction of women on the screen. Hardest hit of all were those who had come to Hollywood from abroad and whose English was inadequate. Others, although North American or British, had voices or accents which belied their romantic visual images. Among those lost to the cinema, or whose careers faded after the coming of sound and who retired or partially retired from the big time, were Pola Negri, Gloria Swanson, Colleen Moore and Vilma Banky. It was a period, therefore, in which many new women stars of distinction appeared, among them Kay Francis, Claudette Colbert, Irene Dunne, Bette Davis, Katharine Hepburn, Barbara Stanwyck, Ginger Rogers, Jean Arthur, Maureen O'Sullivan, Loretta Young, Joan Bennett, Olivia de Havilland and that great debunker of sex, Mae West, while others whose careers stretched back to silent days flowered in the 1930s, such as Myrna Loy, Norma Shearer, Constance Bennett, Carole Lombard and Dolores del Rio. By no means all of these, however, were exactly 'love goddesses'.

Sound meant the ability in actor and actress to handle dialogue; they could no longer be nursed, shot by shot, through situations expressed by means of mime and facial response. Dialogue, and the presence of environmental sound in the form of sound effects, made both characters and environments more real; sound brought the action on the screen closer to the normal experience of audiences, who had accepted most silent films as if they were daydreams. Although most screenplays featuring women stars continued to have much the same qualities as the novelettes and romances on the lending-library shelves, dealing largely with artificially contrived situations involving artificially contrived characters, the presence of dialogue made it necessary for actors and actresses to work with a new dimension of sincerity. They must at least imply they were utterly convinced by what they were doing or saying. It was this high degree of conviction which made them star performers and star personalities. Although there was far more dramatic realism in the better films of the 1930s made in America and Britain than there had been in the 1920s, realism in the modern earthy sense was still almost totally lacking and the stars whose careers we shall be considering and who belonged most significantly to the 1930s appeared for the greater part in films whose stories bore little relation to real life.

The 1930s was also the period when a running battle began between the producers and the American censorship Code, established in 1930 by the Motion Picture Producers and Distributors Association of America and given teeth in 1934 when the Catholic Joseph I. Breen (who had been responsible for drawing up the Code in the first place) was appointed by the MPPDA to license all films on release. At the same time, the Catholic Church formed the notorious Legion of Decency to make public condemnation of films which it considered infringed its narrow concept of morality. Films, therefore, came under fire from both within and without the industry, and this explains the ambivalence' in many productions in which stars such as Marlene Dietrich, Jean Harlow and Joan Crawford appeared after 1934. Films were forced to become moral tracts, with artificial, 'retributive' endings imposed during the last reels for those who during the previous eight or nine had been wallowing in sin and seduction. Many producers chose to circumvent or disregard the spirit, if not the letter of the Code's prohibitions. Technically, the MPPDA had to fine producers $25,000 if they attempted to release a film without Breen's certificate. Censorship had already existed in Britain (though without a written code) since 1913, and many of America's uncensored films had had to be cut in consequence before distribution in this country. Films made in countries like Sweden and France were notoriously free of such inhibitions in sexual matters, but even they, considered in the light of today's productions, were comparatively inhibited. The extraordinary furore caused by the appearance (at some distance) of Hedy Lamarr in the nude in the Czech film *Extase* (1933) is unbelievable today. Strenuous efforts were made by her first husband to buy up all the prints and destroy them. When in 1937 at the invitation of MGM Hedy Lamarr transferred her favours from Czechoslovakia to Hollywood, she was for some while felt to be too hot to handle.

The greater actresses of the silent and sound cinema knew how to convey eroticism without

resort to the obvious. Their appeal was to the erotic imagination. In this lay the art of Garbo and Dietrich. It is the combined art, too, of the American actress, Louise Brooks, and her Viennese director, G.W. Pabst, in the German silent film, *Pandora's Box* (1928); the final scene of her stabbing by Jack the Ripper when in close embrace has an erotic finality which achieves an extraordinary synthesis between what is shown and what is left to be imagined. Rouben Mamoulian's sound film, *Dr Jekyll and Mr Hyde* (1932), seen again today, is astonishingly free with its sexual implications. So ultimately it is by implication, not by direct enactment, that the erotic powers of the film come to fruition.

In a recent book 'On Cukor' by Gavin Lambert, this director makes a similar point, that in the severest days of film censorship the very attractiveness of the players was in itself erotic, and the language of visual implication took the place of direct visual statement; the closing bedroom door was sufficient to excite the erotic imagination. 'It's a cheap cop-out to have unattractive people walking around naked. . . . It seems passionless to me. . . . Sometimes I

Mae West in *Every Day's A Holiday* (1938).

to witness the fulfilment of love upon the screen.

The 1930s was also interesting for what might be termed the social upgrading of the stars. Social 'tone' in Hollywood had already been established in the 1920s by the Fairbanks at Pickfair, and on their various visits to Europe Charlie Chaplin, Mary Pickford, Douglas Fairbanks and Gloria Swanson led the social interchange between the Hollywood élite and the aristocracy of the Old World. Gloria Swanson returned from France a marquise as early as 1925; subsequently, after divorce, the Marquis went on to marry Constance Bennett. Charlie Chaplin's leading lady, Virginia Cherrill, became the Countess of Jersey. Gary Cooper, Sonja Henie, Randolph Scott, Douglas Fairbanks Junior, Johnny Weissmuller all at one stage married into top American society. Even members of the royal families of Europe began to meet socially and informally with the senior film stars, and places such as Pickfair, or Chaplin's house in Hollywood, or the great establishment of San Simeon where William Randolph Hearst lived with Marion Davies (to whom he also gave a fine beach residence) all became recognized centres to which visitors to Hollywood however noble, or intellectually or artistically distinguished, welcomed invitations. The crowning events were not to come, however, until the 1950s, when Rita Hayworth enjoyed a brief, spectacular marriage to Aly Khan (1949–51) and Grace Kelly became Princess of Monaco in 1956. Mostly, however, the celebrated marriages of the period were between people engaged in motion pictures, for example, Norma Shearer and Irving Thalberg, Clark Gable and Carole Lombard, Robert Taylor and Barbara Stanwyck, Laurence Olivier and Vivien Leigh, Walter Wanger and Joan Bennett.

The salaries of certain of the greater stars during the 1930s are on public record. For instance, among the actresses given as earning over $100,000 a year in 1938 were

Claudette Colbert $426,944	Loretta Young $175,060
Irene Dunne $405,222	Bette Davis $143,458
Joan Crawford $305,384	Myrna Loy $140,666
Norma Shearer $300,000	Jean Arthur $136,666
Greta Garbo $270,000	Marlene Dietrich $130,000
Ginger Rogers $208,767	Barbara Stanwyck $117,291
Katharine Hepburn $195,160	

At other times during this period Carole Lombard became worth $150,000 a picture, while in 1931 Constance Bennett earned $300,000 for two films. Mae West earned $326,500 in a single year, only (like other free-lancers) to be out of work the next. Taxation on these sums in the late 1930s lay between 20 and 30 per cent of a major star's salary, according to the officially recognized expenses they incurred.

think there was more sex within the Code than without it.' Elsewhere he says of Garbo in *Camille*: 'She did this memorable erotic thing. She didn't touch Armand, but she kissed him all over his face. That's how you create eroticism. It's the uncensored thought the actor flashes to the audience. Garbo had this rapport with the audience, she could let them know she was thinking things, and thinking them uncensored.' A Garbo or a Dietrich could do far more with a parting of the lips or a movement of the eyes than the young nubiles of today can achieve with the open display of their nudity. One has only to think of Garbo pacing in a last leave-taking the empty bedroom of her lover in *Queen Christina*, absorbing into her memory every detail of its furniture, caressing the bedpost as if it were his body, and leaping on the bed in a silent act of possession, her face reflecting the intensity of sorrow and the ecstasy of pleasure,

How would a high income of $220,000 be spent? The following is an actual breakdown of how one star actress's income was spent in a single year:

Expenditure on her agent, business manager, maid, secretary and publicity representative	$58,600
Taxation, national and State	$75,100
Home	$23,000
Servants, household and domestic expenses	$18,300
Cars	$4,300
Clothes	$6,300
Personal	$5,400
Charity	$1,200
Savings, insurance policies, etc.	$27,300

Such incomes as these were Cinderella figures for girls who had in many cases risen from straitened circumstances in childhood, or who had lived once in actual poverty.

It is no wonder, therefore, that the stars became influential in the lives of their fans, and particularly in the 1930s, prescribed fashions for the world. For example, stylists were happy to meet the demands of millions of girls inside and outside America to have hair like Jean Harlow's shimmering 'platinum blonde' locks in *Hell's Angels* (1930). Later, it was Norma Shearer's hair-style in *Romeo and Juliet* (1936) which had to be copied, smooth on the crown, with curls below the level of the ears. At the same time Greta Garbo adopted the straight hair-style, which hairdressers (to keep themselves in work) adapted to the long, 'curled under' bob. The love-image on the screen became the love-image of real life as girls set out to attract the attention of men who were (they presumed) entranced by the 'love goddesses' of the movies.

Another sophisticated star, Claudette Colbert, with Gary Cooper in *Bluebeard's Eighth Wife* (1938).

Greta Garbo

Even to write about Garbo – the reluctant star of stars – seems like an intrusion on the privacy she so much prizes. Never has an actress of supreme achievement hated so much the excesses in adulation and curiosity her position excites in the press and the public. The most extraordinary thing about her is her ambivalence. Her greatest ambition was to be a good actress, to perform in public; everyone who worked with her testifies to the dedication she brought to her work, striving to give the highest quality of performance to films which were for the most part unworthy of her. She was a great professional, intent always on learning, responsive throughout her career to direction from the men she really trusted, from Stiller to Cukor and Lubitsch, always arriving at the studio fully prepared for the day's work, and noted for the speed with which she complied with the shooting schedules. As soon as she took over control of her own affairs, she proved as hard a bargainer over money and the terms of her contracts as Mary Pickford. Yet she loathed every aspect of the public position which went with stardom – the dressing-up, the premières, the parties, the pressures to meet the socialites of 'high society', the ostentation which the Hollywood way of life imposes, the constant intrusion of the press into her private life. She rejected it completely throughout her professional reign in Hollywood in the later 1920s and in the 1930s.

This ambivalence extended to the exact nature of her femininity, and relations with men. She has never married, and yet it is evident she has through much of her life been very dependent on men – on the men she has liked and respected, that is, all of them men who have in some measure contributed to the fulfilment of her personality, either as an actress or as a very independent woman. For, to understand her, and the extraordinary mystique of her presence on the screen, one must realize that she appeared to have been supremely conscious of what she considered she lacked. Lubitsch, director of her last film but one, *Ninotchka*, has called her, 'the most inhibited person I ever worked with', this when she was a woman in her middle thirties.

Garbo, the cynosure of the world, is a timid, even fearful woman, highly responsive to masculine guidance and even dominance. Yet she is also a very strong woman, standing no nonsense about maintaining her private, even secretive way of life in the very teeth of ruthless curiosity by the press, resisting the pressures put on her by the industry and even, when still only establishing her career in Hollywood, defying for months on end during 1927 MGM's executives until they were forced to agree to her just demands. Similarly, she has rejected all the distinguished and accomplished men who

at one time or another have tried to induce her to marry them, in spite of the attraction, even devotion they have excited in her. Her closer men friends have included Mauritz Stiller, John Gilbert, the Swede Wilhelm Sorensen, the health-food expert Gayelord Hauser, the conductor Leopold Stokowski, Cecil Beaton and George Schlee. Schlee died in 1964 when in Paris with Garbo. Apparently he completely dominated her life. After her husband's death Mrs Schlee (the *couturière* Valentina) is said to have had their house exorcized by a Greek Orthodox priest to rid herself of Garbo's presence.

'I will never marry,' Garbo has often said. Indeed, as with many outstanding actresses, there is a masculine vein in her highly feminine composition – she has referred to herself as a 'bachelor', and her youthful recreations emphasized her solitary ways, walking long distances alone, riding horseback, swimming, sunbathing alone at home. She has tended to fret overmuch about her health. She has little natural interest in the exotic clothes normally associated with her profession, preferring to go about in rough attire which does nothing but help to disguise her beauty. Alexander Walker remarks on her 'long limbs, flat body, largish feet and broad yoke of collar bone', adding that 'from birth Garbo's physique united the two sides of her nature, the feminine and the masculine,' which she was able 'to deploy brilliantly for the emotional effects of her screen acting'. In an article written in 1963 entitled 'Beyond the Boundaries of Sex', Penelope Gilliatt said, 'To play the big parts, actors and actresses have always needed a bit of the other gender in their veins; to feel, in fact, sexual mongrels. Garbo could have played Cleopatra with her little finger. . . . She always seems miles beyond the boundaries of sex, equally and pityingly remote from the men who are in love with her and the women who are vying with her.'

Her background must account for some of this. She was born on 18 September 1905. Her parents had generations of farming stock behind them; her father was an unskilled labourer in Stockholm, and died in 1920. She was born Greta Lovisa Gustafsson. The name Garbo (derived from the Hungarian Gabor) was given her by Mauritz Stiller when she began her career in films. Garbo's impoverished, working-class upbringing in Stockholm, her comparative lack of early formal education, her demanding life first as a lather-girl in a barber's shop and later as a salesgirl in a departmental store, her interrupted training at the Royal Dramatic Academy, combined to make her a shy and nervous teenager, exceptionally dependent on the guidance of Stiller, the temperamental, demanding director of her first feature film, *The Atonement of Gösta Berling* (1924). Stiller had immediate faith in her promise and guided her, a virtual beginner, through a starring role.

Thereafter, for four years in Sweden, Germany and finally in Hollywood Stiller (un-

Right In her first film, *The Atonement of Gösta Berling* (1924). Garbo established herself as a star in Sweden.

married and in his forties) became her supreme mentor and constant companion, at once foster-father, guardian, and artistic dictator. Victor Seastrom (Sjöström), Stiller's fellow director and (with him) virtual creator of Swedish cinema, was among those who believed they were in love. In effect their whole existence was spent together; she (aged little over 20) was accustomed to refer every problem to him. When he died in Sweden (to which he had returned in 1928), and she received a cable from Seastrom telling her of his death in November 1928 while she was actually working on the MGM set, in the words of an eyewitness, 'she turned deathly pale . . . she walked slowly away from us all, as if she were in a trance. . . . She stood there, leaning against the wall with her hands pressed against her eyes for several minutes.' Then she re-covered herself, and returned to work, saying not a word about the cable. According to her biographer, John Bainbridge, the succession of men with whom she was to be closely associated for limited periods through the rest of her life were in effect surrogates for this father-lover-figure who had made her what she was in her extreme youth.

When they were in Berlin, Stiller prepared her daily for her work in Pabst's *The Joyless Street*, and he insisted that MGM include her in his contract when he went to Hollywood in 1926 where, to his acute disappointment, he was not allowed finally to direct her, his methods of work being too chaotic and temperamental to fit in with Hollywood's streamlined mass production. MGM did not know what to do with the beautiful but (they thought) gawky girl he insisted was star material. She was guided through a succession of indifferent films in which she was remarkably successful as the dreamy eyed seductress, parts she despised – *The Torrent* (1926), *The Temptress* (1927), and *Flesh and the Devil* (1927). In the last she played under Clarence Brown's sympathetic direction with John Gilbert, who fell passionately in love with her, while she fell devotedly under his tutelary spell. Their love scenes expressed a passionate, sensual hunger unique in films of the period.

Following this outstanding success, Garbo went on strike and refused to return to work for seven months until her salary was increased from the nominal $600 a week she had been receiving to $5,000. She then appeared with Gilbert in *Love*, an updated version of Tolstoy's 'Anna Karenina'. Then, with other leading men, she appeared as the woman *in extremis* in *The Divine Woman* (supposedly as Sarah Bernhardt, directed by Victor Seastrom), and as a Russian spy in *The Mysterious Lady*. After further indifferent films, she was more fortunate in securing Jacques Feyder to direct her in *The Kiss* (1929), her last silent film, a well-made melodrama of a young wife who kills her elderly husband to protect the boy she has tried to seduce.

She received glowing notices for her films, good and bad alike. It was plain that whether she was a great actress or not she had a radiant

Above In Pabst's story of poverty in post-war Vienna, *The Joyless Street* (1925), Garbo plays a young girl almost driven to prostitution. With Jaro Furth.

Left Garbo and Ricardo Cortez in *The Torrent* (1926), her first American film, in which an attempt was made to cast her as the vamp.

personality on the screen, crowned by a uniquely expressive beauty. The commonplace plots were nothing if not vehicles for 'smouldering passion'. Her lithe, finely muscled grace, the uncontrolled abandonment of her limbs suggested the sensuality that her face aetherialized. Her lips parted, her eyes gazed dreamily into space; she was everywoman awaiting the kiss that would awaken a profound sexuality. She was fortunate to have by now the service of MGM's master photographer, William Daniels, who understood her particular form of beauty and was responsible for the camera-work of all but five of her American films. He knew how to light and shadow her hair (the style of which was constantly changed), the fine bone-structure of her cheeks and her strong jaw-line, the sculpturesque profile, and above all the magnificence of her eyes. As Clarence Brown put it: 'Garbo had something behind the eyes you couldn't see until you photographed it in close-up. You could see her thought. If she had to look at a person with jealousy, and another with love, she didn't have to change her expression. You could see it in her eyes as she looked from one to the other. And nobody else has been able to do that on the screen.'

By now MGM's concern was whether she would achieve the transfer over to sound which so many other major foreign artists were failing to do. A subject was carefully chosen to introduce her deep, husky, yet beautifully toned, sex-laden voice – O'Neill's *Anna Christie*, in which the leading part is that of a prostitute of Swedish origin. Clarence Brown directed the

American version, and Feyder that in German, which Garbo in the end greatly preferred. 'Garbo talks' was the publicity slogan, and the success of this film (the millions of Garbo fans breathing again that she had survived with an added dimension of attraction) led her into another series of tarnished ladies in *Romance*, *Inspiration*, *Susan Lenox – her Fall and Rise* until she reached a further extraordinary peak as the spy in *Mata Hari* (1932) and the suicidal ballerina in *Grand Hotel* (1932).

Garbo in a rare interview said, 'Screen vamps make me laugh tremendously.' What she wanted was to play parts which would have demanded what she held to be real acting quality – among them Shaw's St Joan and an interpretation of George Sand. She would have agreed (most probably) with one of the rare critical statements against the films of this period, made by Mary Cass Canfield in 'Theatre Arts Monthly'. While acknowledging the beauty, finesse and glamour with which Garbo hypnotizes her public, she called her acting, 'a highly finished piece of somnambulism', picturesque but without real or deep feeling. 'This remoteness was . . . your drawback,' wrote the critic in an open letter to her, 'it barred you from being, in any sense, a great actress . . . all your suavity could not conceal the paralysis of your imagination.'

As if taking this address to heart, Garbo's final group of films included her masterpieces:

Right, above Garbo and John Gilbert in *Flesh and the Devil* (1927). She discovered herself with Gilbert, though in her first film with him she still had to play the courtesan.

Right, centre Again with Gilbert as her partner, Garbo played the woman deeply in love in a version of Tolstoy's 'Anna Karenina', *Love* (1927).

Below With Clark Gable in *Susan Lenox – Her Fall and Rise* (1931), one of her outstanding box-office successes.

Above, left Garbo as the notorious spy of the First World War, *Mata Hari* (1932).

Above With Melvyn Douglas in *As You Desire Me* (1932), adapted from Pirandello, which gave Garbo, as a cabaret artist in Budapest, the opportunity to inspire Pirandello to say she played 'at the highest peak of her art'.

Far left In *Queen Christina* (1933). A Garbo masterpiece, this film was directed by one of Hollywood's most imaginative directors, Rouben Mamoulian.

Left Greta Garbo and Fredric March in another version of Tolstoy's *Anna Karenina* (1935).

Queen Christina (1933; director Rouben Mamoulian, and with Gilbert once again), *Anna Karenina* (1935; director Clarence Brown), *Camille* (1937; director George Cukor) and *Ninotchka* (1939; director Ernst Lubitsch – 'Garbo Laughs').* It is always worth noting Mamoulian's remark, so often quoted, that when he was directing the final, most famous shot in *Queen Christina* he told her to stand at the prow of the ship with her mind a blank as she takes her last look at her country, which she is leaving now that her lover is dead. Her face, full of sadness and beauty, has an expression into which each member of the audience can read their own melancholy.

Indeed, Garbo as an actress had this great capacity, unique among the women stars of her time, to suggest emotions which the audience themselves share in creating. Simone de Beauvoir has put this negatively, claiming that Garbo's face 'has a kind of emptiness into which anything could be projected.' Cukor, speaking of her playing of Marguerite in *Camille*, has said, 'She was rather cool, but seething underneath. You know that she is reckless and nothing will stop her.' Thalberg, viewing early rushes, spoke of her as 'unguarded'. Her whole screen personality suggests what the Germans call 'Weltschmerz, world-pain, life-hurt', as Palma Wayne once pointed

Above Garbo as Marie Walewska in *Conquest* (1937), in which Charles Boyer played Napoleon.

Right With Melvyn Douglas in *Ninotchka* (1939). Garbo was able to show her latent sense of humour in the part of a Communist from Russia who learns to love in the style of the West.

* Cukor speaks of Garbo in Gavin Lambert's book, 'On Cukor': 'Garbo's transition [to sound] was very interesting. I remember her in her first sound film, and her voice wasn't flexible at all. Although she had had some theatre training, she wasn't in command of it. Sometimes the gestures and movements were wonderful, but the voice – in *Romance*, for example – just couldn't match them. She spoke English with not the most distinguished accent, but she worked on it, and she has a very sensitive ear, and her speech became an individualised speech. . . . Very few of the great stars of the thirties had been in silent pictures, and very few of them had theatre training. What they had was something quite different, 'personality', that mysterious thing that touches the audience's imagination. Some of the most successful silent screen actors found themselves completely at a loss when they had to speak.'

out. She represents the ultimate sadness, the profound sense of emotional loss and deprivation, of which most feeling people are aware many times in their lives and which this most beautiful woman symbolizes for them with the mature stillness of a sunlit autumn.

John Barrymore, who appeared with her in *Grand Hotel*, said of her: 'Greta is simple and that is her greatest quality. She's also extraordinarily dexterous. She has a very powerful personality which gives her command of everything she does, but she never depends on it. . . . What she does consider is that acting is her job, and she keeps everlastingly at it. It is because she is so completely simple that Garbo bears the unmistakable mark of greatness. . . . She takes us out of ourselves by the mere accident of her presence. It isn't acting; it has nothing to do with acting; it is something which holds us in its spell, a kind of magic.' Clarence Brown, who was six times her director between 1929 and 1937, has called her, 'the prototype of all stars'.

Perhaps this is why she never won an Oscar – she was twice nominated, for *Camille* in 1937, when Luise Rainer won the award for *The Good Earth*, and for *Ninotchka* in 1939, when Vivien Leigh was considered the best for *Gone with the Wind*. These nominations came too late; her kind of 'remote' image was fading. In any case, her films were never the box-office success in America that they were in Europe. David O. Selznick had pleaded with her in 1935 before *Anna Karenina* to do 'a modern subject', with Cukor suggesting *Dark Victory*. But she insisted on the period subject. Her image required, too, the unhappy ending; Selznick

Garbo's performance with Robert Taylor in *Camille* (1936) won her her first nomination for an Oscar.

49

wrote: 'I can't think of a single success in Greta Garbo's long career that has had anything but an unhappy ending.' Like Mary Pickford, she made a grave error in trying to update herself in her last film, *Two-Faced Woman* (1941). But she then wisely decided to retire, at any rate (as she thought) for the time being. She has been near accepting several projects since the war, but for one reason or another (often her own withdrawal) they have never matured. The last to be announced was to have been a brief appearance in a film projected by Visconti, adapted from the works of Proust.

Garbo retired with her fortune – MGM had ended by paying her $150,000 a picture – and remained the enigma she has always been, living as privately as possible but constantly moving about, as someone once put it, 'a hermit about town'. She became an American citizen only in 1951, and resides normally alone in a New York apartment, or in the Swiss ski resort of Klosters, or in the South of France. In 1947, however, Selznick was still dreaming of bringing her back to the screen as Bernhardt, claiming that she 'could be an even bigger star than ever before'.

Cecil Beaton has described her celebrated odd remarks (wrongly thought by her admirers to be witty) as 'wacky', and part of her innate dislike of answering direct questions directly. When he proposed marriage in New York in 1946 (he had first met her ten years before), she refused to take him seriously. He comments on her near-pathological love for secrecy, her fear of going into shops because of the inevitable recognition, her life lived like a recluse. In New York she told him, 'I live like a monk, with one toothbrush, one cake of soap, and a pot of cream. . . . You must realise I am a sad person. I am a misfit in life.' The love-affair, such as it was, faded in 1948, and was only revealed by Beaton when he published his memoirs of this period in 1971. Her beauty, when she does not choose to disguise it, remains. 'She is so beautiful, so beautiful, it's incredible,' said Irwin Shaw after meeting her when she was in her mid-sixties.

To remain a legend seems now to be among her ambitions: she is acutely conscious of her status, and realizes that to return to the screen would most likely break the spell. The re-release of the best of her old films has been miraculously successful, though she has gained nothing financially from this. However, this scarcely matters, for, as her biographer Bainbridge has said, she is 'several times a millionaire' in dollars.

Greta Garbo (seated) with Constance Bennett, Melvyn Douglas and Robert Sterling in *Two-Faced Woman* (1941). Under George Cukor's direction, Garbo tried yet again to masquerade as a comedienne.

Marlene Dietrich

Maria Magdalene Dietrich was her name at birth, a Berliner born on 27 December 1901.* Middle class, the daughter of an officer in the Royal Prussian Police, she was well educated, including learning to speak English and French. Her adolescent ambition was to be a concert violinist, but a muscle defect in her arm led her to fulfil her second ambition, to act. Since her mother (a widow) opposed this idea, she changed her first name to Marlene, a combination of Maria and Magdalene. Money was short with the collapse of the mark in 1923, and she had to earn her living; after a period in the chorus-line in Hamburg, she was finally accepted by Max Reinhardt as a student in the Deutsch Theaterschule, playing small parts in their full-scale productions in the early 1920s and at the same time earning money playing similar roles in films. Her favourite part during this early period was that of a judge's mistress in Joe May's film, *Tragödie der Liebe* (1923).

In 1925 she married May's assistant, Rudolf Sieber, by whom she had her daughter, Maria,

in the same year. Then she returned to the stage and screen, playing small supporting parts for Pabst (*The Joyless Street*, 1925), Robison (*Manon Lescaut*), Korda and others. She appeared with Willi Forst and Harry Liedtke in increasingly sophisticated films, including Robert Lande's *Ich küsse ihre Hand, Madame* (1929), while on the stage she appeared very successfully in Shaw's 'Misalliance' and 'Back to Methuselah'. 'She became the prototype of the *diable de femme*', said Victor Barnowsky, the Reinhardt of Vienna, where Dietrich had become as well known as in Berlin. 'More beautiful than ever, strikingly like a portrait by Toulouse-Lautrec,' he remarked after seeing her at a costume ball. And Elisabeth Bergner said of her, 'If I were as beautiful as Dietrich, I shouldn't know what to do with my talent.' Her beauty, including that of her legs, was holding back her development as an actress. Trained from childhood to hide her feelings, what Sternberg was later to admire was her coolness, her disdain, her aloofness in the presence of men.

By 1929 she was well established in both theatre and film, usually playing women who lived freely. She was successful in Reinhardt's production of the American musical, 'Broadway' (1927) in which she starred. She appeared as a wealthy American woman in Reinhardt's production of George Kaiser's revue, 'Zwei-Krawatten', with songs by Mischa Spolianski, the part in which Josef von Sternberg saw her when he came to Berlin under contract to UFA to make *Der Blaue Engel*, starring Emil Jannings. 'Here was the face I had sought,' writes Sternberg in his autobiography, 'Fun in a Chinese Laundry'. He insisted on having her, though Jannings, he says, 'violently opposed' it. When tested, Sternberg wrote, 'she came to life and responded to my instructions with an ease that I had never before encountered'. In the film, under his direction, she stole the picture from Jannings in the part of Lola-Lola, the vicious cabaret-singer who destroys the staid old professor by casting her perverse physical spell upon him without any sign of pity or feeling. She sings in her low-pitched, haunting voice: 'Falling in love again; Never wanted to; What am I to do; I can't help it.' Sternberg wrote of her:

Despite her melancholy, she was well dressed and believed herself to be beautiful, though until this was radically altered by me she had been photographed to look like a female impersonator. . . . Never before had I met so beautiful a woman who had been so thoroughly discounted and undervalued. . . . I did not endow her with a personality that was not her own. . . . I gave her nothing that she did not already have. What I did was to dramatise her attributes and make them visible for all to see.

Before the screen test so amusingly described by Sternberg, she had seemed utterly listless. He had acquired a ferocious reputation in Hollywood for his treatment of his players, but she neither knew of this nor seemed anyway

Opposite page Marlene Dietrich, with (inset) the poster for a box-office disaster, von Sternberg's *The Scarlet Empress* (1934).

Marlene Dietrich in *The Blue Angel* (1930), where in her first film for von Sternberg, she was, in her own words, 'made over' for the screen.

to care. But when he treated these tests as if they were shots for a real film, giving her careful direction, she immediately responded. 'I put her into the crucible of my conception,' says Sternberg, 'pouring lights on her until the alchemy was complete.' While the film was being made, she followed his instructions implicitly, referring herself to the relationship between Liza Doolittle and Professor Higgins. Nevertheless, she found the work agonizing and was convinced her interpretation of Lola-Lola would be the end of her. The film was made simultaneously in German and English, Dietrich and Jannings playing in both, but finding the English difficult. Sternberg made her create a languorous, cruelly erotic woman in an environment steeped in sexual imagery: high heels, black tights, silk top hat, she represented glamour shining in the sleazy surroundings of a backstage cabaret. One

critic called her, 'a new incarnation of sex'. But her German producers let their option on her services lapse. Paramount was quick to make her an offer, and (after much deliberation) she arrived in Hollywood early in April 1930. Sternberg had returned to Berlin to fetch her.

There now began the close creative relationship which was to persist through five years and six more films. The success of *The Blue Angel* was followed by that of *Morocco* (in which she was a cabaret-singer once again, playing opposite Gary Cooper and Adolphe Menjou). With ebullient irony Sternberg describes how Dietrich made herself his slave and boasted to the press about her subservience to him on the set. As her reputation reached the heights, so her self-acknowledged dependence on her mentor seemed to grow. She received an Oscar nomination for *Morocco*.

In Hollywood, which she did not like, she

Marlene-**DIETRICH**

THE SCARLET EMPRESS

FROM THE DIARY OF
CATHERINE THE GREAT

Above As the woman who resorts to prostitution to save the life of her husband, Dietrich displays her celebrated legs in *Blonde Venus* (1932).

Left Dietrich as the exotic courtesan, Shanghai Lily, with Clive Brook in *Shanghai Express* (1932).

Opposite page Garbo as *Camille* (1936), in which under George Cukor's direction she gave one of her finest performances.

spent all her time with Sternberg, on the set and off, which led to the usual gossip, though both of them were married. However, her one private desire was to return to her husband and daughter in Berlin, which she did, only to be fetched back by Sternberg to make *Dishonoured*, in which she was to play a spy in a Viennese setting, starring with Victor McLaglen. Every detail of movement, interpretation, lighting became a matter for intimate conference. Everything was calculated, and Dietrich learned from him exactly how she should be lit. Sternberg built up the Dietrich legend in press interviews: 'Dietrich is the most intelligent woman I have ever known, and the most

Right Dietrich as the future Catherine the Great with John Lodge and C. Aubrey Smith in *The Scarlet Empress* (1934).

Below As another seductress, with Lionel Atwill as her prey in *The Devil is a Woman* (1935).

Below, right Dietrich with Gary Cooper in *Desire* (1936), which gave her the opportunity to show her capacity for comedy.

thoughtful. . . . Marlene has the feeling that there is nothing so important as the things we aré working upon.' On the screen, he built her image round seduction – furs, veiling, sequins – and he put her in this, as in other films, in uniquely exotic settings. He clothed her in eroticism and created her mystique in light and shadow. He was, he says, 'editing a human being'. Paramount by now were paying her some $125,000 a film.

Though her husband and child were now with her in Hollywood, Dietrich had to face being cited in a divorce suit initiated by Sternberg's wife, demanding £120,000 for alienation of his affections and for libel. Dietrich, however, contested this, and the case was dropped since the allegations were found to be based on the fabrications of a journalist. These problems arose after the completion of *Shanghai Express* (1932), with its Chinese setting and with Dietrich as a European courtesan meeting an old flame (Clive Brook) on the train, and saving him from torture at the hands of Chinese insurgents by offering her body to their leader

Dietrich with Mischa Auer and Broderick Crawford in *Seven Sinners* (1940), a satire on the conventional South Seas picture.

With Melvyn Douglas in *Angel* (1937), another comedy, in which she was successful.

(Warner Oland). *Shanghai Express* proved the greatest commercial success of the Sternberg-Dietrich pictures; she appeared with a spotted veil casting its pattern over her face like a photographer's gauze.

Dietrich and her husband were as close as ever, but in professional terms she continued to express her utter dependence on Sternberg, refusing to work with any other director. His extravagance worried Paramount as much as the thought of losing her, since she now rivalled Garbo herself in popularity.* Her clothes offscreen (she dressed often in shirt, tie and pants) set a new, sophisticated style for women, supplementing her occasional male attire in films. As with Garbo, the male touch in her nature became part of her star quality. Professionally she was in a strong position, and could state her terms. 'I am happy with Mr Sternberg because I trust him. How do I know what another director could do with me?' she said. 'I am devoted to him, and I made the devotion myself because my brain told me to.'

In her next film for Sternberg, *Blonde Venus* (1932), she is again the cabaret-singer, playing with Herbert Marshall as her husband and Cary Grant as her wealthy lover. Its alleged immorality (the husband accepts her back without the obligatory retribution) alarmed the

studio. A dispute with the executives was resolved, but the strain was beginning to tell on both director and star. *Blonde Venus* did not do as well as the previous films at the box office. Then, urged by Sternberg himself as well as the studio executives, she ventured to work for another director. This was Rouben Mamoulian and the film *Song of Songs* (1933), in which she is a beautiful peasant girl who models a nude statue for the sculptor played by Brian Aherne and afterwards becomes a sophisticated society woman and entertainer.

With her next film, Dietrich (now in her early thirties and one of Hollywood's highest paid stars) returned to Sternberg for the most idiosyncratic and extravagant of his productions, *The Scarlet Empress* (1934), their joint masterpiece, projecting in romantic, highly stylized vein the career of the German girl Sophia Frederica, brought to Russia to marry the half-wit Grand Duke Peter, only to lose her initial innocence in the decadent Russian Court and seize the throne for herself to become Catherine the Great. The film is one of the most exotic ever photographed in Hollywood, and her performance is as stylized as the settings. But this film, like *The Blue Angel*, has a lasting quality, unlike most of her other early films which date in spite of her languorous beauty to the point of absurdity, though their stories have to be accepted as a masquerade to frame her exoticism. Needless to add, *The Scarlet Empress* failed at the box-office – it had no recognizable place in the cinema repertory of its day. Sternberg's last film with Dietrich, *The Devil is a Woman* (1935), a period Spanish story in which she appeared as a seductress in a succession of extravagant costumes, fared no better. As Sternberg put it himself: 'My being with Miss Dietrich any further will not help either her or me.' Nevertheless, *The Devil is a Woman* has remained Dietrich's own favourite film: 'Because I looked more lovely in that film than in any other of my whole career.'

Dietrich now had to face working with other directors, and come down to earth from the ivory tower into which her work with Sternberg had increasingly enclosed her. Her producer now was Lubitsch, her director Frank Borzage, and she appeared as a sophisticated jewel thief in *Desire*, with Gary Cooper. This restored her to her public, and was successful. But her career became now more miscellaneous – she appeared in a series of films which aimed at romantic popularity, the spectacular *The Garden of Allah* (1936), the spy story *Knight without Armour* (made in England for Korda, with Jacques Feyder directing) and, back in America, Lubitsch's film *Angel* (light and sophisticated). In America at this time she was considered 'box-office poison'. Nevertheless, for *Knight without Armour* she received $450,000, and Feyder said of her, 'She has great charm, and uses it with stunning virtuosity.'

After a period of rest and travel, she updated herself by appearing in 1939 as proprietor of a saloon in a Western, *Destry Rides Again*; in this she sang, 'See what the boys in the back

Above, left Dietrich with Jean Gabin in a French production, *Martin Roumagnac* (1946).

Above Dietrich as the film star, with James Stewart in *No Highway* (1951), adapted from a story by Nevil Shute.

Left Dietrich in Fritz Lang's Western *Rancho Notorious* (1952).

room will have', and had a vicious fight with Una Merkel on the bar-room floor. Her fee for this film is said to have been only $50,000. By now her very real sense of sardonic comedy was beginning to assert itself, and she entered fully into the American scene as the ribald Frenchie. After playing an entertainer in *Seven Sinners* (1940), she passed into the hands of another great director, René Clair, for the romantic comedy, *The Flame of New Orleans* (1941). She was to appear in a succession of films of little importance but which kept her in the public eye mainly as a saloon girl, including three with John Wayne, *Seven Sinners* (already mentioned), *The Spoilers* and *Pittsburgh* (both 1942). In a revue-type film, *Follow the Boys*, she was sawn in half by Orson Welles, and in *Kismet* she danced as a nautch-girl, covered in gold, while after the war she dyed her skin to appear as a gipsy in *Golden Earrings*. Nothing could be more different from the Sternberg Dietrich.

Her husband kept himself now in the background in California, while she lived in New York; the high life she has since lived in America and Europe is not to his taste. She remains devoted to her family, but her image and inclination demand male friends. Her selection of escorts in show business as noted by her biographer, Leslie Frewin, makes an interesting cross-section – they have included at various times Maurice Chevalier, John Gilbert, Douglas Fairbanks Junior, Michael Wilding, Noël Coward, John Wayne and Jean Gabin. Apart from show business, her friends have included Remarque, the novelist, and Sir Alexander Fleming, the scientist. With Gabin, she made her first French film, *Martin Roumagnac* (1946); this was not successful, but *A Foreign Affair* (1948), directed by Billy Wilder, gave her an opportunity to bring Lola-Lola up to date. She was a night-club singer in post-war Berlin. She followed this with an

Dietrich with Vittorio De Sica in *The Monte Carlo Story* (1957). She played a confidence trickster in this Italian-American co-production directed by Sam Taylor.

appearance as a stage-singer in a film for Hitchcock, *Stage Fright* (1950), and she was a famous film star in *No Highway* (1951), with James Stewart, both films made in England. She was successful in Fritz Lang's *Rancho Notorious* (1952), and picturesquely decadent in Orson Welles's heavily stylized *Touch of Evil* (1958). In 1957 she had made another film for Billy Wilder, *Witness for the Prosecution*, and she played a German widow in Kramer's *Judgment at Nuremberg* (1962).

With films becoming few and far between and for the most part of little interest, she turned in 1953 to playing in real life what she had so often done on the screen – she became a cabaret entertainer whose most notable song is, perhaps, 'Where have all the flowers gone' with its romantic, nostalgic lament for youth and love. 'I had no desire to be a film actress,' she has said in an interview in 1964, 'to always play somebody else, to be always beautiful with somebody constantly straightening out your every eyelash. . . . When I sing my songs, then I am an actress. I act the lyrics.' After initial appearances at Las Vegas and the Café de Paris in London, which were both highly successful, she adopted this as a new career in which she was, as in films, always the professional, the embodiment of glamorous show business. She masquerades in fabulous dresses, such as the famous rhinestones creation of 1954 or the dress of the million stitches and 227,000 beads, together with a 12-foot train made up of the breast-feathers of 300 swans, which she wore at Las Vegas. 'I dress for the image,' she says. Privately, she prefers jeans: 'I dress for what I am doing.' In the midst of it all, she keeps her sense of humour. As Zukor has said of her, she is 'indestructible because above all she is an individual.'

Jean Harlow

Jean Harlow (born Harlean Carpentier) was an only child of what became a broken marriage; her father was a dentist in Kansas City, Kansas. She was born on 3 March 1911, and had a privileged upbringing, though her parents separated when she was ten and her mother married again – an immigrant called Marino Bello. The whole family, including her grandparents, appear to have concentrated over-much on bringing up 'Baby', as they called the beautiful child. They were determined she should be well educated. She was sent eventually to an exclusive 'finishing' school in Illinois, from which she ran away at the age of 16 to marry a boy of 21 from Chicago – Charles (Chuck) Fremont McGrew, whom she had met at a dance. So in 1927 she became Harlean Carpentier McGrew. The marriage, conceived on the spur of the moment, did not last long; the

young couple went to live in Los Angeles, but so did Mr and Mrs Bello. The errant Harlean and her husband separated in 1929, and finally divorced in 1931.

Once in Hollywood, Harlean became an extra in films. She used her mother's maiden surname, calling herself Jean Harlow. She was short, 5 foot 2½ inches in stockinged feet, but she had a fine profile, strong jaw-line, prominent cheekbones and blue eyes. The most striking thing about her was her silky, white-blonde hair, and her magnificent breasts, which she normally left unconfined by a brassière. She appeared, rather scantily clad, in two Laurel and Hardy films of 1929, *Double Whoopee* and *Bacon Grabbers*, and she even had a small part with Clara Bow in *The Saturday Night Kid*. When she was still only 19, she had the luck to be spotted by an agent, Arthur Landau, and contracted through him to Howard Hughes to replace Greta Nissen in the remake with sound of *Hell's Angels* (about the British Royal Flying Corps) starring Ben Lyon and James Hall. For this she received $250 a week.

With her looks and figure she could not help being type-cast as the 'vamp' swathed in revealing gowns, and she made an instant mark with her performance in *Hell's Angels* as the girl with the abundant 'platinum' hair who makes love to every man she meets. She delivered several 'near-the-knuckle' wisecracks with zest – they had to be cut in England. *Hell's Angels* was primarily a spectacle of war in the air produced and directed by Hughes, the 24-year-old Texan oil millionaire and air ace. Hughes's acceptance of Jean to star in one of the most sensational films devised to launch the new era of sound was a fantastic break for her, especially as she attended the premières at Grauman's Chinese Theater in Hollywood as well as on Broadway. Her stunning appearance – in the film she wore a backless evening gown which was cut virtually to the waist in front, and what was left to cling, clinging – was a scandalous success. One English critic called it, 'the most disclosing raiment that has ever been seen on the screen'. Her remark to one of the fliers, 'Will you excuse me for a moment while I slip into something more comfortable?' was received with outraged delight. She was regarded by the press as 'sexquisite'. No one bothered whether or not she was an actress, or whether her frankly mid-western American accent and throaty laugh suited what purported to be an English setting.

At this stage Jean played the languid vamp with well-outlined eyebrows, sloe-eyes, dark eyelashes and shadowed eyelids. She was to liven up considerably later, her natural intelligence revealed through comedy. But meanwhile she set an immediate fashion for platinum blondes, and just as immediately she was typed by Hollywood as the new vamp for sound films – with hard-boiled sex-appeal and talking 'slanguage'. She established her own down-to-earth wit in press interviews; she became notorious for her spicy epigrams and saucy come-backs to questions. And she posed end-

Above Jean Harlow with
Douglas Gilmore and Ben
Lyon in *Hell's Angels* (1931)
an American-made story of
the British Royal Flying
Corps of the First World War
— in which she played a
highly sexed interest in the
lives of the fliers.

Right In *Iron Man* (1931),
Harlow played the sex-
obsessed wife of a boxer,
Lew Ayres.

lessly for photographers, in and out of everything.

Under contract now to Howard Hughes, she was hired out in 1931 to appear as a siren in a spate of films, which at least kept her image before the public and the press – *The Secret Six*, *The Iron Man* (with Lew Ayres), and with Spencer Tracy in *Goldie* (in which she was referred to as a 'tramp', considered at the time to be the first use of this term of the 1930s on the screen). She was a gangster's moll in William Wellman's *Public Enemy* (1931, with James Cagney), but the film which advanced her was

Frank Capra's comedy, *Platinum Blonde* (1932), the picture which led to the founding of a chain of platinum-blonde clubs in American cities, while women were invited by speech-trainers to come and learn to 'talk as tough as Harlow'. In this film, however, Loretta Young manages to oust her from her man, a reporter; Harlow's acting as an aristocratic girl who is the 'delusion' in the reporter's life is described by one critic as 'ludicrous', but her name was a draw. Nevertheless, Capra was quoted as saying, 'No one has ever realized Jean Harlow's potentialities. . . . Here is a personality which

Above Harlow moved increasingly in the direction of comedy, which became her best vein in film. With Chester Morris in *Red Headed Woman* (1932), where she played the vamp.

Right Jean Harlow and Robert Williams in Frank Capra's comedy *Platinum Blonde* (1931), where she loses the man she has set her heart on.

Far right, above Sexual comedy became her metier. With Clark Gable in *Red Dust* (1932) she played the imperturbable, quick-tongued blonde in a circus world.

Far right, below In *Dinner at Eight* (1933), she plays the over-indulged wife of Wallace Beery's tycoon, a witty, wise-cracking performance.

* Irving Shulman's distasteful biography, *Harlow*, became a best-seller in 1964, which says little for either the author or his readers. It is written like fiction with invented dialogue and concentrates on the Bern affair, and it lapses into the luridly sexual at every opportunity.

will be more intriguing and more dominating if it is not exaggerated by make-up and costuming.' And Marie Dressler (who befriended her) told her, 'You must show them you're an actress before they burn you out.' She advised her to develop a lighter touch, and make entertaining personal appearances.

Accompanied by her mother and step-father, she went on tour during the winter of 1931–32, and again proved sensational merely by appearing in public. Her agent managed in 1932 to negotiate somewhat better terms for her; Howard Hughes parted with her contract to MGM for $60,000, plus the right to use her in two films within five years at her regular salary, which MGM agreed should be $1,250 increasing to $5,000 a week over a seven-year period. Yet her talent continued to be wasted in poor films until her capacity for comedy was finally realized. She began to play the vamp for comedy in the tough MGM film, *Red-Headed Woman* (in which she wore a flame-coloured wig) and to better effect in Victor Fleming's *Red Dust*, with Clark Gable, who was also her leading man in *Hold Your Man* (1933).

At MGM she met a shy, middle-aged executive of 40, Paul Bern, a man considered to be 'cultured' and 'scholarly', and as far as women were concerned, something of a recluse; he had secured her the coveted part in *Red-Headed*

Woman. They married quietly in July 1932. The marriage had every appearance of succeeding (in spite of their seeming incompatibility) when suddenly, only two months later, Bern's naked body was found lying in front of a mirror in his dressing-room. He had been shot through the brain. The facts behind the tragedy were that the marriage had been very unhappy. Bern's death left a mystery about which speculation was rife, only to be increased when a woman calling herself Dorothy Milette arrived from New York to claim she was Bern's wife. Then she disappeared to San Francisco, where she committed suicide.

Bern left a note for Jean saying, 'this is the only way to make good the frightful wrong I have done you and to wipe out my abject humiliation'. It was widely assumed from this that he had been impotent. Jean resolutely refused to explain what the words meant, ostensibly to protect Bern, and she went back to work at the studio in *Red Dust*. It had to be assumed Bern had committed suicide, though murder had been suspected, and Jean's reputation suffered, though her box-office value was not, as MGM had feared, impaired.* She appeared with a roster of great stars in Cukor's

Dinner at Eight, playing a former hat-check girl married to a roughneck millionaire. Cukor was delighted with her, exclaiming, 'She's simply eating up the scenes.' Indeed, she handled the excellently characterized dialogue with immense attack, standing up magnificently to Wallace Beery's brutal weight – 'Ah don't feel so good'; 'Ah'm gown to be a lady if it kills me'; 'Mah skin's so delicate ah don't dare expose it', and so on.

She followed this with *Bombshell* (1933; director Victor Fleming) with Franchot Tone. The film was a satire on the Hollywood scene: here she was at her best, playing a star surrounded by adorers and dogs and plagued with the demands put upon her by her publicity agent (Lee Tracy), which continually frustrate her desire to marry and become a simple wife and mother. Her cameraman on this and other pictures since *Red-Headed Woman* had been Hal Rosson, and he was the next man to fall in love with her, leading to another disastrous marriage, undertaken on the spur of the moment with typical Harlow impetuosity. Eight months later she divorced him, the reason given that he was jealous and morose, and that 'he read in bed'. Rosson, like Bern,

Right In *Blonde Bombshell* (1933), she made fun of her own image in the Hollywood setting.

China Seas (1935), like *Red Dust* before it, starred Clark Gable opposite Jean Harlow as a tropical 'tramp'.

was the quiet, studious type, and sixteen years older than Jean. So Jean returned again to her mother's home. She had led a life of pleasure up to the time of her marriage, including much gambling, and she went on strike for more money – writing a novel in the interval. Her rate for the job at the studio was increased to $1,500 a week.

Now that her vein was securely comedy, the lighter films followed: *One Hundred Per Cent Pure* and *Reckless* (in which she first appeared with her next love, William Powell, with whom she also starred in *China Seas* and *Libelled Lady*). After numerous studio conferences she had changed her image by wearing a wig – a gamble that succeeded. She appeared in 'brownette' for *Riff-Raff* (with Spencer Tracy) and *Wife versus Secretary* (1936, with Clark Gable).

The cosmopolitan William Powell, suave, perpetually the gentleman, became Jean's acknowledged escort and lover. He had played villains until he, too, changed his image for *The Thin Man* series, in which he starred with Myrna Loy, the two making up a sardonic husband-and-wife detective team. Now at last Jean had paired off with someone of similar temperament to herself – easy-going and pleasure-loving; neither had been successful in marriage, and they did not attempt it now with each other. They decided on 'friendship', and indeed 'eloped' in 1936.

While making her last film, *Saratoga* (1937), with Clark Gable, Jean fell seriously ill. Her health had never been good, and she suffered persistently from influenza. Her successive illnesses during 1936 and 1937 had been kept from the public, for sex goddesses should never be ill. Her final illness was reported to be uremic poisoning; she died with her family and William Powell by her bedside. In the mortuary, her body was laid out in a clinging dress of petal pink silk, and she was buried in a silver-bronze coffin which cost an estimated £1,000. Large crowds gathered for the funeral; there was a mass expression of grief, and what her first biographer, Dentner Davies, calls 'funeral glamour' second only to Valentino's hysterical interment in 1926. *Saratoga* was completed with a double in Harlow's part, and a morbid public flocked to see it.

In all, Jean is computed to have earned a million dollars from films, yet she died leaving only some $25,000, in spite of the fact that she had inherited money from Bern. But she had been a great spender, and she had also been responsible for keeping her family in luxury. She had been popular in the studios, and liked by everyone. The best assessment of her, as a talented personality star and at least a potential comedy actress of skill, is perhaps that made by Alexander Walker in 'Sex in the Movies', and Francis Wyndham has said of her: 'It is quite possible for a woman to be sexually promiscuous and at the same time capable of emotional loyalty – the basic combination for Harlow's form of sentimentality. . . . She was racy, unpretentious, human and rather hard. Like all great mythological figures, she seemed to have her cake and eat it; a good-bad girl (or was she a bad good girl?), she enjoyed the best and the worst of both worlds.'

Again playing for comedy, she appeared with Spencer Tracy and William Powell in *Libelled Lady* (1936).

Joan Crawford

Joan Crawford's legend is indestructibility. Her screen career spans the half-century from the 1920s. She was born Lucille LeSueur in 1904, and raised in Kansas City, Kansas, child of a broken marriage, and living in straitened circumstances. Used to a hard life since childhood, she had worked as a domestic help away from home, and as a waitress and store assistant before training to be a dancer. She was 'the girl third from the left in the back row' in a Broadway musical, 'Innocent Eyes' when she was seen by Harry Rapf of MGM and given a screen test. So at the age of 17 she was summoned to Hollywood on New Year's Day 1925 and given a six-month option at $75 a week. For her test she had been asked to walk to a fixed mark, look full-face to camera, then profile, next look sad, mad, questioning, wistful and coy – the standard feminine range. She had been successful.

She and Myrna Loy, another beginner, were part of the female décor in *Pretty Ladies* (1925), Joan's first appearance on the screen. She got her new name of Joan Crawford as the result of a national magazine contest inviting the public to invent a name for an MGM star, and it was used in the first film in which she had a considerable part, Irene in *Sally, Irene and Mary* (1925), with Sally played by Constance Bennett, and with Edmund Goulding directing – a director from whom she was to learn a great deal. Her fine figure and athletic poise had also led to endless posing for MGM publicity photographers, and she was well known for being a 'hotcha kid' on Hollywood's Montmartre dancefloor, famous for her Charleston. She was a 'hey-hey girl'. Meanwhile, she appeared in numerous supporting parts in films starring Norma Shearer (for whom she doubled), Jackie Coogan, Harry Langdon (in *Tramp, Tramp, Tramp*), Charles Ray, Lon Chaney, John Gilbert and William Haines. She even appeared with Tom Mix in a Western and worked for many of the most professional directors of the period – William Wellman, Edmund Goulding, James Cruze, Jack Conway, and Tod Browning. With Lon Chaney she played a gipsy girl in *The Unknown* (1927) and began to understand the seriousness of acting in watching Chaney's feats of physical endurance in the parts he was called upon to play, in this case an armless knife-thrower. Her six-month contract had been renewed, with a salary rising to $100 a week. From 1925 to 1928 she received, in fact, a thorough grounding in all aspects of studio work. She also learnt, she has said, 'to keep my vitality undiluted on the screen, never to let down for a moment'.

The film that made her image was *Our Dancing Daughters* (1928), in which she asked for and got the part of Diana, a Clara-Bow-type flapper who 'dances herself into a frenzy while the saxes shriek and the trombones wail'. She was, she says, 'a girl drunk on her youth and vitality'; she acquired 'flamboyant personality'. She had to be noticed.* Harry Beaumont, the director of a predominantly young cast (Dorothy Sebastian, Johnny Mack Brown, Anita Page, Nils Asther), told them to let themselves go and rely on instinct, an early example of improvisation. Crawford stood out from among the rest, and she at last saw her name in lights outside the theatres. She began to attract shoals of fan mail, and MGM doubled her salary. She was now able to earn $500 a week. A sequel, *Our Modern Maidens*, appeared in 1929. In this she starred with Douglas Fairbanks Junior, and they married in June 1929 after a year and a half of courtship.

In her first sound film, *Hollywood Revue* (1929), she tap-danced and sang, 'Gotta Feeling for You'. But her urge now, in her mid-twenties, was to secure more dramatic roles, and raise herself from being type-cast as the flapper, as she continued to be in *Our Blushing Brides* (1930). 'I wanted to be a serious dramatic actress,' she writes, 'I was Mrs Douglas Fairbanks Junior.' Douglas induced her to read Wells, Shaw, Ibsen, Proust, and she had to endure the social routine of Pickfair. She managed to secure, again by pressing for the part herself, the starring role in *Paid* (1930; director Sam Wood) which Norma Shearer (Mrs Irving Thalberg) had been forced to relinquish through pregnancy. She was a clerk in a store who is 'railroaded to prison' and then seeks her revenge; this gave her some chance to show her ability to act an emotional part. She wore no make-up.

The sheer professionalism of Joan Crawford is what marks the progress of her career. She is completely alive to the nature of failure and success. The films in which she appeared, both the successful and the unsuccessful, were novelettish, and most of what she had to enact involved characters and situations so contrived and artificial they would seem merely ludicrous today. However, the successful star was one who, like her, got the most out of the material presented to her. Her professionalism was to bring strong conviction to each part in turn, as she worked for a variety of directors, and teamed with a succession of male stars with whom the public liked to see her. Clark Gable as the gangster was so successful in his scenes with her (as a socialite newspaper reporter) in *Dance, Fools, Dance* that MGM had her next film, *Laughing Sinners* (1931) remade to present them as a team: he became a Salvation Army man concerned to rehabilitate Crawford's prostitute cabaret girl. They were to appear in eight films together, including *Possessed, Dancing Lady* and *Chained*. 'This magnetic man had more sheer male magic than anyone in the world and every woman knew it,' she says. And she admits she was in love with him, and he with her. He was married, while she was divorcing and unhappy.

Crawford regretfully divorced Douglas Fairbanks during 1933, and in 1935 married another

Opposite page A 1963 portrait from the later period of Joan Crawford's career, which began with her playing frenetic flapper-girls and now has her playing dramatic 'horror' roles.

Right Joan Crawford as the flapper in *Our Dancing Daughters* (1928), one of the parts that established her in this role.

Below In *Our Modern Maidens* (1929) she starred with Douglas Fairbanks Junior who was to be her husband.

highly cultured man, Franchot Tone, who appeared in several of her films and who was a dedicated stage actor from the Group Theater. This marriage foundered in its turn in 1936, owing largely to career conflict. In both her marriages she lost babies through miscarriages, and after the break-up of her second marriage she adopted two children. In 1942 she married a young actor, Phillip Terry, but this marriage too did not last, and she adopted two more children.

This Modern Age (1931), which followed *Laughing Sinners*, was criticized as being 'a shop-girl's delight', but when the film made money Crawford countered by saying, 'There must have been a lot of shop-girls, bless 'em.' Crawford had a professional interest in her fans and fostered them; she knew a star's success depended on their mass-loyalty. She counted the letters she received, replying individually until the sheer mass of them defeated her – 900,000 by 1938.

The period 1932–33 was to be a peak in her career, starting with the celebrated composite story film, *Grand Hotel* (director Edmund Goulding), in which she played what she calls a 'whore-stenographer', Flammchen, and *Dancing Lady* (director Robert Z. Leonard). In this she starred opposite Gable. They had a notable scene together, she as a hungry, but lady-like chorine being entertained at a restaurant by Gable, as a surly producer. *Rain*, her other film

of the period, was considered less successful – 'I gave a lousy performance', she says. But at the end of 1932 she was voted third-top money-making star of the year, beating Greta Garbo, whom she greatly admired, and with whom she had hoped to act in *Grand Hotel*, but they appeared in different stories.

A second director from whom she was to learn much was George Cukor, celebrated as a director of women, and who, in the comedy *No More Ladies* (1935) insisted she gave more meaning to her lines. The film was a comedy (she had appeared rarely in comedy, and was interested to go further in this field). He gave her 'the roughest time I've ever had'. She was good enough, however, for Cukor to ask for her again for another, later comedy, *Susan and God* (1940). She was now frequently playing society women, even if they were somewhat of a shop-girl's idea of a lady, as some critics maintained. She had been dressed to kill by Adrian in W. S. Van Dyke's *Forsaking All Others* (1934) and the flamboyant make-up she had used in past films, emphasizing her wide mouth and mesmeric eyes ('broad, bold and blatant', as she put it), gave way to a more lady-like appearance.* But it is evident she has a very strong face, with a powerful jaw-line and straight nose, and it is this, combined with the resolute character she achieved in maturity that has made her the established career woman she is both on the screen and off. According to Johnny Arnold,

In *Montana Moon* (1930), Crawford played opposite Johnny Mack Brown.

* 'Great fashion-designer Adrian for 14 years designed everything I wore in pictures and most of what I wore personally. The clothes he created had great impact on the styles of the whole country. He toned me down in line and colour and gave me the tailored look women have treasured ever since.' ('A Portrait of Joan').

Opposite page Betty Grable (second from right, above) with Iona Mackenzie, Sheree North and Janice Carroll dancing the honky-tonk number from *How To Be Very Very Popular* (1955). Marilyn Monroe (below) shows her figure off to equal effect in a 1953 pin-up shot.

of MGM's camera department, her face had been 'built'. She gave her finest performance to date under Clarence Brown's direction in her only historical film, *The Gorgeous Hussy* (1936), in which she plays an innkeeper's daughter who became the power behind the throne of President Andrew Jackson (Lionel Barrymore) in America of the early 19th century. Again, she wore little make-up, and the strength in her face was brought out by George Folsey's camerawork.

Not all her films were successful; indeed in 1935 she received the dreaded 'box-office poison' label from the 'Independent Film Journal', along with, rather notably, Garbo, Dietrich, and Katharine Hepburn. Nevertheless, Louis B. Mayer, who had always been generous to her, re-contracted her for a further five years at $1,500,000, the requirement being she should make three pictures a year. She appeared, however, in little of distinction until *The Women* (1939; director George Cukor), in which she was happy to play 'the bitch', Crystal, the salesgirl who steals Norma Shearer's husband and wears a $40,000 wardrobe. In *Strange Cargo* (1940) she once again wore no make-up; this was her last film with Gable; she was a dance-hall girl in the tropics involved with convicts on the run. The best film of her last period with MGM was *A Woman's Face* (1941), which Cukor directed; it concerned the total change in character which comes over a woman when the scars on her face are removed by a beauty surgeon. Cukor rehearsed the emotionalism out of her in order to achieve precisely the right level of restraint, and gave her, she claims, a new self-confidence as an actress.

She left MGM after having been under contract to the studio for 17 years. She was 34. The parting was mutually agreed. She felt in need of a rest and a change of direction, and she voluntarily gave up a contract with Warners, which they had taken out for only one-third her MGM salary. She gave herself up to war-work and a domestic life. Apart from a guest appearance as herself in *Hollywood Canteen* she did nothing until *Mildred Pierce* (1945), directed by Michael Curtiz, for which she won her Oscar in 1946. It was strikingly photographed by Ernest Haller, who worked with equal distinction on her next film, *Humoresque* (1946), and was probably her most responsive cameraman. In *Mildred Pierce* she played the ex-waitress mother who kills for the sake of her worthless daughter; in *Humoresque* she was brilliant as a dipsomaniac society woman, patroness of a violinist of humble origin (John Garfield); at the end she commits suicide in high style by walking into the sea. On the strength of this film Warners signed her securely at $200,000 a film for seven years, from which once again she sought release after appearing in such formula films as Otto Preminger's *Daisy Kenyon* (1948), *Flamingo Road*, and *The Damned Don't Cry* (1950).

She went back to MGM (and colour film) for *Torch Song* (1953), and to Republic for the

Above left Crawford as another flapper in *Our Blushing Brides* (1930).

Above centre Crawford with Norma Shearer (right) in *The Women* (1939).

Above With Kent Smith in *The Damned Don't Cry* (1950), a dramatic role of her later period.

Far left With Lester Vail — the scene from the negligée ball in *Dance, Fools, Dance* (1931).

Left In *Possessed* (1947), Crawford played one of the heavier dramatic roles in which Warner Brothers decided she should star.

Below With Jack Carson in *Mildred Pierce* (1945), the film that won her an Oscar.

Above Crawford's development as a dramatic actress
led her into the genre of
horror in *Whatever Happened
to Baby Jane?* (1962), with
Bette Davis.

Right Crawford and her
lover Jeff Chandler in *Female
on the Beach* (1954), in
which she believes he is
planning to murder her.

'psychological' Western, *Johnny Guitar* (1954), directed by Nicholas Ray, in which she played Vienna, a sharp-shooting saloon-proprietor who ends up in a full-flowing evening gown playing the piano alone while her saloon is under siege. Rumour (or was it publicity?) made her out to be difficult on the set in this and other films, and liable to provoke her fellow artists if she did not like them; she was attacked in the press for this. She expresses resentment at these allegations in her autobiography. After working for the first time with Robert Aldrich as the career woman in *Autumn Leaves* (1956) and in England with David Miller in the successful film, *The Story of Esther Costello* (1957) she withdrew again from films in order to promote a new and supplementary career as wife and business associate of Alfred Steele, Chairman of the Board of Pepsi-Cola, who in 1956 had become her fourth husband. She was terrified of flying, but accepted it at once in his company. There is an interesting chapter in her memoirs in which she explains how, as a career woman, she learned to adjust to him as a fully dedicated career man – 'Tough as he was, strong and professional, this man needed a wife. . . . Alfred Steele was the tenderest of men and I the gentlest of women.' After his sudden death in 1959, she joined the Board of the company and became its official hostess, though at the same time returning to the screen and undertaking additional work on television.

It was in 1962 that she made the remarkable come-back in Robert Aldrich's 'horror' film, *Whatever Happened to Baby Jane?* (1962), in which she appeared with one of her oldest rivals at Warner Brothers, Bette Davis. This ghoulish picture (in which her playing was far more restrained than that of Bette Davis) was a resounding success. But once again, success typed her, this time for horror films, though she had to retire through ill-health from the successor Aldrich had designed for her and Bette Davis, *Hush, Hush, Sweet Charlotte*; she was replaced by Olivia de Havilland, it was said to the relief of Bette Davis and the rest of the cast.

Although the few films she has appeared in since have been minor ones, her urge to work seems undiminished. Her raw, abounding energy has carried her though well over 80 films, while her screen career spans some 45 years. 'They've said I worked with the diligence of a ditch-digger being the great star,' she has said. 'They're right.'

Crawford and John Ireland in *Queen Bee* (1955), in which she returned to comedy, though still as a potential murder victim.

THE NINETEEN FORTIES

This was a watershed period for the cinema, a period of acute transition coupled with easy access to audiences rising during and immediately after the war to unprecedented totals, especially in Britain. It was the last decade in which the medium was to enjoy freedom from the competition of television, yet it was also the decade of dislocation through the war. British production was reduced in quantity but immeasurably improved in quality. The war concentrated and refocused the outlook of British and American film-makers; their films became dominated by war themes balanced by wholly escapist stories designed to take the minds of people, Service folk and civilians alike, off the subject of war. The major film industries of France and Italy were absorbed into a Europe dominated by Nazi Germany, with many great directors and stars living and working in exile. The second half of the decade was concerned with the aftermath of war – with rehabilitation, with recrimination, with the need in the younger generation to look ahead for something better and freer than the dark days of their childhood or adolescence. No one wanted to be identified with the horrors of the immediate past.

One actress typified the romantic melancholy of these times in France – Arletty, star in the films of Marcel Carné and Jacques Prévert which immediately preceded the period of invasion by Germany and spanned the years of occupation. Other actresses came forward in America and Britain to add their talents to those already established, most of them appearing in films of distress – separation through war and its dangers, or foundering through misplaced love. The stars of the cinema were changing, becoming more natural, more real in their emotional needs and expression, more approachable, even more domesticated. The 'love goddesses' with their other-worldly 'mystique' were perceptibly passing, to be replaced on the screen by women in uniform, women facing the dangers of war service or concerned with maintaining their families and homes in wartime. Garbo withdrew from films; Dietrich entirely changed her image. This was the beginning of the period of heightened naturalism, and even cynicism, seen not only in the war film but in such varied films as *Citizen Kane* (1941), *The Maltese Falcon* (1941), *Sullivan's Travels* (1942), *Farewell, my Lovely* (1944), *The Lost Weekend* (1945), *Mildred Pierce* (1945), *The Best Years of our Lives* (1946), *On the Town* (1949), *All About Eve* (1950) and *Sunset Boulevard* (1950). This was in addition to the romantic bravura of *Gone with the Wind* (1939), *For Whom the Bell Tolls* (1943) or *She Wore a Yellow Ribbon* (1949). New writers and directors with a special skill in handling actresses were coming into prominence, among them John Huston, Elia Kazan, Joseph L. Mankiewicz, Billy Wilder, Tennessee Williams and Fred Zinnemann, and in Britain David Lean and Carol Reed.

So the key actresses began to change in style and personality, along with the change in the characters they had to interpret: Rosalind Russell (the business-like career woman), the genteel ladies of Joan Fontaine, Olivia de Havilland, Irene Dunne, and the usually demure Deborah Kerr. They were all mature (if still young) women, workers in a film industry which was itself rapidly maturing along with the tastes of its audiences. And there were others, mostly newcomers, who helped create the image of the period: Lauren Bacall, who changed her appeal from siren to assured woman of the world after marrying Humphrey Bogart, the 'peek-a-boo' Veronica Lake, the aggressive Susan Hayward, and Betty Hutton, Linda Darnell, Lana Turner, Maureen O'Hara, Paulette Goddard, Greer Garson, Judy Garland, Rita Hayworth, Gene Tierney, Jane Russell, Barbara Stanwyck, Ava Gardner, Margaret Lockwood and Jennifer Jones. Among the recorded salaries were (in 1946):

Bette Davis	$328,000
Deanna Durbin	$325,470
Betty Grable	$299,333
Ann Sheridan	$269,345
Rosalind Russell	$190,104
Rita Hayworth	$94,916

The cinema is capable of sustaining any demand put upon it by its creators, the film-makers and their audiences. It had begun on the simplest level in such films as Mary Pickford had made, which were readily understandable by the least demanding or sophisticated of audiences. Yet even on the simple level, a great art was being born, and the best work of Greta Garbo, though she still appeared in screenplays which were little more than romantic novelettes, sustained an art of acting which satisfied the highest standards. The more complex or intellectualized film is not necessarily better art merely because of its complexity. But with the coming of sound, speech added immeasurably to the great possibilities for the interpretation of human nature already realized in the silent

film through absorbing details of behaviour and facial expression. The film had moved a significant stage forward, though it was to take a decade and more to realize what was involved in the new art of screenwriting, the subtle balance between the opportunities acquired through the addition of dialogue and sound and the opportunities of observed action and re-action already known in the silent film. Writers, directors and actors all had to share in this understanding, and it was the 1940s which saw

Above One of the most sympathetic of Hollywood's stars, Joan Fontaine won an Oscar for her performance as the unhappy wife in Hitchcock's *Suspicion* (1941), with Cary Grant.

Left Lauren Bacall changed her screen personality to a more complex, highly individual woman when playing in a series of films with Humphrey Bogart, with whom she is seen here in *Key Largo* (1948).

Below Considered one of the most beautiful of the screen's 'love goddesses', Ava Gardner does her stint as the inevitable vamp with Burt Lancaster in *The Killers* (1946).

the more general realization of this balance in films which, at their best, were more mature in subject and treatment than those of the previous decade.

So the goddesses had finally come to earth, and were on the whole far better and more interesting for it. One goddess especially, Jane Russell, promoted, like Jean Harlow, by Howard Hughes, appeared in a film which anticipated the 1950s – *The Outlaw* (1943) – and was held up for three years by the violent opposition through censorship not only to its frank sexuality but to the crudely devised publicity campaign, including lurid posters, which heralded its much-postponed appearance. Jane Russell, earth goddess, was a sign of the times to come.

Arletty

Arletty, the Garbo of France, was born in 1898 at Courbevoie in the Auvergne, the district associated with Maupassant's story, 'Mont Oriol'. According to her own account, her name, Arletty, comes from Maupassant's heroine, Arlette. Her real name is Arlette-Léonie Bathiat. Her father was a miner, and she remembers him as strong and gentle, but he died in 1910.

She had no initial ambition to be an actress; she simply learned shorthand and typing and went to work in an office until the First World War claimed her as a worker in the Darracq armament plant which manufactured shells. After this she became a mannequin and an artist's model, and graduated in 1920 to the theatre, playing every kind of role, eventually appearing in Paris with Raimu and Spinelli. She also performed as a singer and dancer in films from 1930, following her appearance in the operetta 'Yes' at the Théâtre des Capucines. This led on to supporting parts in films, such as Jacques Feyder's *Le Grand Jeu* (1934) and *Pension Mimosas* (1935) and Sacha Guitry's *Faisons un Rêve* (1936); she played the blackened Queen of Abyssinia in Guitry's *Les Perles de la Couronne* (1937). Other early films were *La Chaleur du Sein* and the gay *Circonstances Atténuantes* (1939), both with Michel Simon. At the same time she was still working hard in the theatre, which remained her primary profession; she appeared in both the play and the film, *Fric-Frac* (1939; director Claude Autant-Lara) also with Michel Simon, with whom she had to ride on a tandem both on the stage and in the film. Later, in 1941, she played Josephine in *Madame Sans-Gêne* to Robert Dieudonné's Napoleon. Dieudonné was already famous for his Napoleon in Abel Gance's celebrated silent film of 1927.

In Arletty's case, it is interesting that there were to be two, quite different images on the screen – the fresh, carefree, witty plebeian woman of *Fric-Frac*, and the other-worldly image of mysterious, surpassing beauty for which she is mostly remembered as a film actress, which came when she starred in the most celebrated films in France of the late 1930s and the occupation period, those of Marcel Carné and Jacques Prévert – *Le Jour se lève* (1939), *Les Visiteurs du Soir* (1943), and *Les Enfants du Paradis* (1944), films conceived in the style of 'poetic realism' so much in favour with the French during the pre-war and occupation periods. She had also appeared in a supporting part in Carné's earlier film, *Hôtel du Nord* (1938), an episodic, tragi-comic study showing a cross-section of working-class life in Paris, a film which also had its poetic overtones. But in *Le Jour se lève* she was able to fulfil the part of a woman belonging to a world which blended Carné's impressionistic realism of the streets, seedy hotels and shabby back-street theatres and Prévert's melancholy concept of defeated idealism and beauty.

As Clara, the oppressed and bitter mistress of the demented Valentin, Jules Berry's sadistic dog-trainer who incarnates bestiality and a fatalistic acceptance of evil, Arletty represents a woman who longs for contact with real love represented by Jean Gabin's hunted workman. In the film she stands for profane love, an easy, friendly though somewhat ambivalent and fatalistic acceptance of pleasure as it comes. She plays with a superb casualness, establishing a special presence and personality in the film, assured and beautiful. But above all she embodies sheer, mature physical beauty, a sympathetic contrast to the younger heroine of the film, the innocently pretty flower-seller of Jacqueline Laurent. Whereas most film stars reach their full stature comparatively early, Arletty reached hers only when she was already forty.

When the Carné-Prévert films were seen at the close of the 1930s and during the occupation in France, and when *Les Visiteurs du Soir* and *Les Enfants du Paradis* were released outside France immediately after the war, in 1946, the effect was phenomenal. They seemed to interpret the spirit of the period, and Arletty herself became the feminine 'presence' in them, at once remote and earthy, embodying a mature physical acceptance of love while remaining in some measure aloof from it, tender but at the same time free from entire involvement. In *Les Visiteurs du Soir* her beauty is at its most impassive. Set in a castle in 15th-century France, two emissaries of the Devil disguised as itinerant troubadours appear in order to destroy the happiness of the two young people at their betrothal feast. But they are not, it would seem, true lovers, and one of the emissaries, Gilles, finds an ideal love in the act of seducing the girl. Arletty, as Dominique, Gilles's devilish companion, is able to destroy the pious father of the girl; she ensnares her victim through the obsession her hypnotic beauty inspires in him, folding him in a destructive enchantment. This remains one of Arletty's favourite films.

But the film which has made the most lasting impression is *Les Enfants du Paradis*, Carné's near four-hour spectacular re-creation of Paris in the early 19th century, and in particular Paris of the popular theatres of the Boulevard du Temple. The *enfants du Paradis* are the theatre-lovers in the gallery. In this film Arletty plays Garance, a woman of the booths and theatres who is loved by many men, good and bad alike; she accepts them easily as lovers but with a quality of enigmatic remoteness which keeps her independent. Her true love is Baptiste, the mime too shy, withdrawn and filled with melancholy idealism to enjoy other than a tortured love for her. The film ends in tragedy and frustration. Again, it is the bad who prevail, imposing suffering upon the good. In this film Arletty is supreme in the near-symbolic, feminine character she had by now come to embody, a character more subtle in its implications than

Above Arletty and Bernard Blier in *Hotel du Nord* (1938) in which she worked for the first time with Marcel Carné, the director who was to make her an international star.

Right Arletty with a youthful Fernandel in *Fric-Frac* (1939).

Above Arletty with Jean-Louis Barrault (right) in *Les Enfants du Paradis* (1944).

Far left Arletty with Alain Cuny in *Les Visiteurs du Soir* (1942), the first of her films directed by Carné during the Occupation.

Left Arletty in the production of *Les Enfants du Paradis* (1944).

that created by Garbo, but in many ways similar in its projection of a 'feminine mystique'.

Like Garbo, Arletty refused to live the life of the film star offscreen. She dressed entirely to suit herself, often in the simplest of clothes. She did not marry, though she had many escorts; again like Garbo, she preferred to live independently, in effect on her own. Her known admirers included Sacha Guitry and the late Aga Khan. But she lived more for her profession, both theatre and film, than for anything else, and she educated herself to become a woman of considerable taste and distinction, with a genuine, unassuming love for the arts, She became one of the most admired women in Paris, loved alike for her beauty and her sunny, unaffected temperament, taking life as it comes. She was constantly photographed, and notable portraits were painted of her in profile by Van Dongen. Her one notable love-affair, which brought her great suffering, was with a Major-General in the German Air Force whom she met in Paris in 1941, and who was drowned in Africa shortly after the war. Although the relationship was kept concealed, she was charged with collaboration after the war, but the case was dropped.

Following the war, she appeared in many more films and stage productions, one of the most notable being in the French stage version of 'A Streetcar named Desire', in which she played Blanche. In a brief memoir written in 1948, she mentions with amusement that she was among the first actresses to appear nude on the screen – in *Le Jour se lève* and again in *Les Enfants du Paradis*. She was as little concerned about this a quarter of a century ago as the actresses of today, such as Glenda Jackson. If the part demanded it, she complied. She was also prepared to play the lesbian in the film of Sartre's play, *Huis Clos* (1954), directed by Jacqueline Audry, and in 1961 she had the part of a Frenchwoman, Mme Barrault, in the international production, *The Longest Day* (1961), concerned with the first phase in the liberation of France on D-Day. Although in 1967 she accidentally blinded herself, she has very courageously continued to work whenever the opportunity arose, in spite of failing health.

Arletty as the Lesbian in Sartre's *Huis-Clos* (1954), with Gaby Sylvia.

Vivien Leigh

Vivien Leigh (Vivian Mary Hartley) was born in Darjeeling of well-to-do parents on 5 November 1913. Her parents were French and Irish, a point she had in common with Scarlett O'Hara. Her father was a stock-broker, and her infancy was spent in India. After the war, she received a privileged education in England at the Convent of the Sacred Heart at Roehampton; a fellow boarder was Maureen O'Sullivan at this very strict and very upper-class Catholic establishment. From the age of 13, her education followed an international pattern; she studied languages in the South of France, Italy and Switzerland, becoming a sound linguist in German and French, and able later to dub her films in these languages. Her mother encouraged her interest in art, and she was sent to 'finishing' schools in France and Germany where her interest in music and drama was roused. She returned to London and studied briefly at the Royal Academy of Dramatic Art. Then in December 1932 she married, when only just 19, Leigh Holman, a rising young barrister. At the age of 20, in 1933, she had a daughter, Suzanne.

However, married life and an elegant home in Mayfair proved insufficient for her. She continued to have voice training under Elsie Fogerty and hankered after the theatre and the independence an earned income (if only amounting to 'pin-money') would bring. She had a will of her own and a unique, delicate beauty. Through her social position (she had been a débutante and was presented at Court after her marriage) she achieved some small parts in minor films which she enjoyed as much for the social life with the other girls as for the experience involved, and she put herself in the hands of an agent, John Gliddon, specially interested in placing society girls in theatre and film. On his advice she adopted the name Vivien Leigh, derived from her own and her husband's names.

She was virtually without training; it was her looks and refined voice that brought her the many minor parts she played in film and theatre until the stage-producer, Sydney Carroll, who had real faith in her potential talent, gave her a leading part in May 1935 in Ashley Duke's comedy, 'The Mask of Virtue', which made her famous in London overnight. Margaret Lane described her at the time as a 'tiny, slender-boned little creature with the grey eyes and delicate, heart-shaped face'. She was 21.

Her new-found stardom (based on beauty, intelligence and charm of personality more than on any developed acting skill) won her a contract from Alexander Korda's London Films worth £1,500 rising to £1,800 a year for an annual six-month period of work in the studio. This appeared encouraging, but Korda failed to produce her any part in a film until *Fire over England* (1937). Laurence Olivier, whom she had already met and with whom she was falling in love, was to be in the cast, and they played lovers. As a result, Olivier asked for her to play Ophelia to his Hamlet in Tyrone Guthrie's Old Vic production which was taken to Elsinore in June 1937. When they returned from Denmark, Olivier and Vivien Leigh finally decided to give up their marriages and live together. After the divorces were finally through, they were able to marry in 1940.

From 1937, parts came much faster for her on both stage and screen; for example, in the film, *Dark Journey* (1937, with Conrad Veidt), *A Yank at Oxford* (1938, with Robert Taylor) and *St Martin's Lane* (1938, with Charles Laughton). Meanwhile Olivier had gone to Hollywood to play in *Wuthering Heights* and, unable to exist away from him, Vivien followed to America. It

was the greatest stroke of luck in her career. The coveted part of Scarlett O'Hara in Selznick's production, *Gone with the Wind*, still remained uncast after a search lasting two years; all the seemingly suitable names in Hollywood had been rejected and the film, to be directed by George Cukor, had actually gone into production. Selznick describes how his brother Myron, a leading agent, introduced her to him while she and Olivier were watching the shooting of the burning of Atlanta. 'I want you to meet Scarlett O'Hara', he said.

Cukor has claimed she was eventually accepted not only because she turned up in Olivier's company at the studio at the right time, but because of her unusual beauty. She was (Cukor has said) 'fresh and not shopworn', and unknown to American audiences; 'It was the type we were looking for.' Also, she cost little: $15,000. But her voice ('piping', Cukor called it at first) was a problem. However, she was not merely well bred; she was utterly unsentimental, and she proved capable of giving a wild-cat touch which came out in the test. The days of waiting for the studio's

decision were agonizing, more especially because Guthrie wanted her back urgently in London to rehearse for Titania in his stage production of 'A Midsummer Night's Dream' at the Old Vic. But she got the part, and signed a seven-year contract with Selznick, which was later to prove restricting.

The full glare of publicity fell on Vivien when on 13 January 1939 it was announced this virtually unknown girl was to be Scarlett O'Hara. The film was a great venture for Selznick, and there was considerable nervous pressure on all involved, including Olivia de Havilland and Clark Gable, who was (according to Cukor) lacking in self-confidence as an actor. No less than eleven writers had been engaged on the script. Cukor himself was dropped after only two weeks, to Vivien's consternation. The succeeding director, Victor Fleming, was a favourite of Clark Gable, but he collapsed after six weeks' work and was replaced for a while by Sam Wood. In secret, Vivien received coaching by Cukor in the character (whom she did not like), and she showed many signs of fatigue and strain during the prolonged

Opposite page Vivien Leigh and Flora Robson in *Fire Over England* (1937).

Vivien Leigh in the spy story *Dark Journey* (1937) with Austin Trevor (right).

Opposite page Vivien Leigh on set as Scarlett O'Hara in Gone With the Wind (1939).

Vivien Leigh as the street performer who makes her name through the influence of Charles Laughton in St Martin's Lane (1938).

Right Vivien Leigh as the flirtatious wife of a don with Maureen O'Sullivan in A Yank at Oxford (1938).

period of shooting which the film required.

Vivien studied the Southern accent assiduously as well as the character of Scarlett O'Hara. 'I lived Scarlett for close to six months from early morning to late at night. I tried to make every move, every gesture true to Scarlett and I had to feel even the despicable things Scarlett did were my doing,' Vivien said, looking back on the film. Cukor has commented, 'The part of Scarlett has a very earthy, primitive, tough side and a kind of ruthlessness that was in contradiction to her looks and delicacy.' He says he had to use 'four letter words to get something very primitive and shocking in her'. Recently, in recorded talks with Gavin Lambert, Cukor spoke very highly of her: 'She was often underrated because she was so beautiful. . . . She was a consummate actress anyway, hampered by beauty – and as a person the complete romantic. She had this great talent for creating beauty around her, she made exquisite gardens, she dressed ravishingly, she had true breeding.' When Lambert breaks in to remark that her obsession with beauty was a compensation for

'disorder under the surface,' Cukor agrees. 'You felt something tragic even when she was at her happiest.' He adds, 'She was Rabelaisian, this exquisite creature, and told outrageous jokes in that voice cool and pretty enough to make you weep.' Vivien Leigh told Gavin Lambert that Cukor 'laid out for her the part . . . in the tests and rehearsals and talks'. Selznick describes her at work: 'Vivien made no secret of her opinion of certain scenes as she went along during the 122 days she was on the set . . . she groused plenty: before a scene, she would be muttering deprecations under her breath and making small moans . . . the situation was stupid, the dialogue was silly. . . . And then at a word from Victor Fleming . . . she would walk into the scene and do such a magnificent job that everybody on the set would be cheering.' It won her an Oscar. Vivien was to make two more films in Hollywood during this difficult period, with Britain and the Commonwealth fighting the war alone, and America still technically neutral: Waterloo Bridge (with Robert Taylor) and, with Laurence Olivier, Lady Hamilton (That Hamilton Woman) – the latter becoming, oddly, a top favourite alike with audiences in Russia and with Winston Churchill. At last, on 30 August 1940, she and Olivier were free to marry. Their film completed, they returned to London at the end of the year when it was under heavy bombardment from the air. Olivier, by now a trained pilot, joined the Royal Navy Volunteer Reserve; Vivien played Jennifer on the stage in Shaw's 'The Doctor's Dilemma'. This production was so successful that it had a six-month provincial tour and a run of over a year in London. It led to her personal contact with Bernard Shaw, and his acceptance of her as Cleopatra in the film which was to be made of Caesar and Cleopatra (1946; director, Gabriel Pascal), plans for which were started as early as

1943. It was not a film she enjoyed making. Work began shortly after D-Day following a strenuous three-month tour in an all-star company sent out to entertain the Forces in North Africa. Meanwhile, Laurence Olivier had completed *Henry V*.

It has to be remembered that after her success as Scarlett O'Hara, Vivien was one of the most wanted stars in Hollywood.* She was under contract to Selznick, who had prevented her from playing the Princess in *Henry V*. But she resolutely refused to return to America during the war period – she wanted to be with her husband and to work in England; a lawsuit finally resolved the matter in Vivien's favour, and she was able to fulfil her ambition to appear in Olivier's stage production of 'The Skin of Our Teeth'. She came into her own as the charming minx, 'part gamine, part woman, a comedienne, an artist', wrote Beverley Baxter. It took Noël Coward to perceive her strength – 'She has a body like swansdown and the constitution of a GI on leave.'

While Laurence Olivier was making *Hamlet* he was knighted, and Vivien became Lady Olivier; they set up home in Notley Abbey, near Aylesbury. This they turned into a place where they could constantly entertain guests at weekends. She was now working on *Anna Karenina* (director Julien Duvivier, with Ralph Richardson), a film she came to regard as a mistake. She also developed symptoms of tuberculosis, and was forced to rest, which frustrated her boundless energy and her great skill as a tireless hostess. In 1948, she toured Australia and New Zealand with Olivier in a repertory of plays.

Olivier was determined to use every opportunity he could to work alongside her and extend her dramatic skill and range in the theatre. In the Old Vic season at the New

Theatre (1948–49) she played both Antigone in Anouilh's play and Lady Teazle with outstanding success. Her voice remained a problem, and she was constantly in training; while good for films, her vocal range lacked strength, flexibility and projection in the theatre. From the Old Vic she moved to playing Blanche in Tennessee Williams's new play, 'A Streetcar named Desire', directed by Olivier in London. The part was immensely trying and demanding, but exactly the kind of acting challenge she most enjoyed. As an actress she was analytical, dedicated, ceaselessly curious about the potentialities of a part; she developed into a supreme technician of the theatre. Acting never came easily or instinctively to her, as it did very often to Olivier, superb technician though he is. She always had to work for it. The play had an eight-month run in London, and she was invited to be the star in the film version, directed by Elia Kazan. Brando, as leading man, was not yet sufficiently known as a film star to carry the picture.

Kazan has said of her performance: 'The way

* As if to counterbalance this amazing good fortune, she and Laurence Olivier had sunk all their savings while still in the States on a stage production of 'Romeo and Juliet' which proved a disaster, to Selznick's chagrin, since he had permitted her to do this. 'This endeavour seriously damaged her career,' he writes. She wanted in 1940 to act for the Theater Guild, but Selznick forbade this (as he did in the case of Ingrid Bergman) under the terms of his seven-year agreement.

Above Vivien Leigh as Scarlett O'Hara and Clark Gable as Rhett Butler in *Gone With The Wind* (1939).

Left Vivien Leigh and Thomas Mitchell in *Gone With The Wind* (1939).

Leigh and Robert Taylor in the romantic story *Waterloo Bridge* (1940), in which once again true love is sullied by degeneration into prostitution.

presence eased the inevitable tensions she always experienced through hard work and concentration. And as Lady Olivier she appealed to the social set in Hollywood; she was always a highly social woman, witty, entertaining, though her candour could upset people.

The Oliviers returned to London at the end of 1950. Her success in *Streetcar*, with which she had been preoccupied now for two years, resulted in her second Oscar. Now she felt ready to extend her range even further by playing in 1951 the two Cleopatras, Shakespeare's and Shaw's, in Olivier's twin productions on the stage in London and New York. It was a feat of transposition, alternating Shaw's petulant, dangerous 'kitten' with Shakespeare's maturely passionate but devouringly unstable dark lady.

The destruction of the St James's Theatre, which she and Olivier had made their theatrical centre for eight years, came as a severe blow to them. She demonstrated in public for the preservation of this century-old building, and even caused a sensation by protesting from the gallery of the House of Lords when it was in session. This and other strains, such as the persistent rumours she and Olivier were contemplating separation, had led to her breakdown while working on the very indifferent

she did it at first, scaled to the stage, seemed rather more artificial to me. By the time we got into the last weeks she was superb.' She and Brando, he knew, were 'two different kinds of animal', their 'technique as different as can be. . . . She came from another civilisation, from another way of life, and somehow that fitted into the way the characters were.' There were problems at first in transmuting her performance from the London to the American atmosphere, and to Kazan's rather different conception of Blanche; he prefers her in the latter part of the film. But Vivien herself has said, 'It took three months to make the film and I loved every second.' Kazan's intense, hard-driving methods of work suited her, and she came to terms with Brando, whose tough, brusque but also wary attitude she found at first 'affected', whereas he felt the same about her lady-like good manners. But 'she never stopped trying to be excellent,' said Kazan. 'She was determined to be wonderful, and she was.' She excited everyone's admiration; the rest of the cast had played *Streetcar* on Broadway for 18 months under Kazan's original direction, with Jessica Tandy as Blanche. Kazan observed afterwards, however, that he considered Vivien's talent to be a limited one; what he admired was her intelligence, honesty and forthright opinions. 'We were both highly strung and temperamental people with strong tastes and with likes and dislikes, but somehow we got very close when we knew each other.' She thought of herself primarily as a stage actress; it was Kazan's opinion she was better in films. Fortunately, Olivier was also in Hollywood working on *Sister Carrie*, and his

Above Vivien Leigh and
Laurence Olivier in *Lady
Hamilton* (1941), the highly
romanticized version of the
Nelson-Hamilton story which
became a box-office success
in both America and the
Soviet Union.

Left Leigh and Flora Robson
in Bernard Shaw's *Caesar
and Cleopatra* (1945).

Right Leigh in another adaptation of Tolstoy's *Anna Karenina* (1948).

Below Vivien Leigh came from Britain to star in Kazan's film version of Tennessee Williams's *A Streetcar named Desire* (1951), the film which made Marlon Brando into an international star.

film, *Elephant Walk* (1954). She was, says her biographer Gwen Robyns, in a 'manic-depressive' phase, and her mental collapse came after the second week in Hollywood following a month on location in the heat of Ceylon. In a state of total distraction she was flown back to London in the care of Olivier, who had gone to Hollywood to fetch her.

This was not the first, nor the last time she had suffered serious relapses of this kind, which led to utter bewilderment, inability to recognize even close friends, periods of intense weeping, resistance to help, even violence. They came when her energy finally overtaxed her strength. She suffered from periods of intense depression.

Four months of treatment and rest and she was eager to work again, and appeared, as immaculately beautiful as ever, with Olivier in Rattigan's play, 'The Sleeping Prince'. But in spite of this success (with Vivien yet again looking 20 when she was 40, the essence of guileful innocence) their careers and their temperamental demands seemed to be drawing them apart. She had shown during their season at Stratford (1955) that she could not always include Shakespeare in her compass; she was not really a 'classical' actress. She had also appeared in Anatole Litvak's film version of *The Deep Blue Sea* (1955) with Kenneth More, whose naturalistic warmth as Hester's feckless lover stole the film from her over-cold handling of this pathetically needful woman. Then, in 1956, when Olivier was battling through an agonizing production of *The Prince and the Showgirl* with Marilyn Monroe, Vivien lost through miscarriage a baby conceived when she was 43. It was a tragic blow for them both.

Olivier was at the height of his career, working intensely in both theatre and film. He and Vivien were under constant pressure to comment on their private relationship. By 1959 they were all but separated, working and living in different spheres. In 1960 she was receiving shock treatment in New York while playing in 'Duel of Angels', and it was in this year that the break finally came in the marriage which had lasted over 20 years, and a close association of 25. Notley Abbey had been sold. After the divorce in December Olivier married Joan Plowright. In Cukor's view, Vivien never recovered from her separation from Olivier.

Now, with a life to live entirely on her own, she accepted a part she had at first refused when approached by Tennessee Williams – the lead in *The Roman Spring of Mrs Stone* (1961), her first film for six years. Mrs Stone is a beautiful actress facing the onset of age and a life which has begun to drift in the decadent society of Rome. She played this under José Quintero's direction with her usual meticulously disciplined but naturalistic technique, appearing opposite Warren Beatty (a Method-style actor) as her gigolo-lover. The film was criticized because she gave it too little emotion, too little compassion for this lonely woman with needs similar to those of Hester. But at least she looked the part, being elegantly decked out by Balmain.

After this she turned again to the stage – to a tour, as sole star, at the head of an Old Vic company visiting Australia, New Zealand and Mexico. She also starred in 1963–64 in the American production of 'Tovarich', but had to return to England in a state of breakdown. She was becoming somewhat difficult to work with; she could be 'bitchy' to those she disliked, but also generous and kind to those she favoured, including certain stage-door fans whom she came to know personally. She was essentially – in spite of her temperamental lapses and difficult nature – a kind, considerate, and gracious woman.

Her last film also dealt with the theme of a beautiful woman escaping the onset of age and the lack of anything left to live for, this time an alcoholic divorcée, in Stanley Kramer's *Ship of Fools* (1965). The film was episodic, over-laden with characters, and pretentious, but she gave an effectively ironic performance as a woman forced to recognize the truth about herself.

She died on 7 July 1967, aged 53. No one, not even those closest to her, knew she was so ill with tuberculosis. She was at the time rehearsing with Michael Redgrave in Albee's play, 'A Delicate Balance', but she had been unwell, complaining of exhaustion. She died quite suddenly near midnight, alone in her room, and she was discovered dead by the man who had tried to bring her some comfort during the lonely years, the actor John Merivale.

Above Vivien Leigh as the alcoholic divorcée in *Ship of Fools* (1965), with Nigel Patrick.

Left With Kenneth More in Anatole Litvak's film version of Terence Rattigan's play *The Deep Blue Sea* (1956).

Betty Grable

Betty Grable (Ruth Elizabeth Grable) was born on 18 December 1916 in the German section of South St Louis, USA. Her mother Lillian Grable, had entertained ambitions to become an actress, and was determined her daughter should succeed where she had failed, so she set her on the usual path for a girl – the dancing school. Her father, a book-keeper at the time of her birth, progressed and enabled his daughter to receive a good education. So ambitious was Lillian for her daughter that in the late 1920s she took her to live in Hollywood, leaving her husband back in St Louis, which led ultimately to a break-up of the marriage.

Betty was sent in her early teens to schools in Hollywood which offered training for work in films, including dancing. Their efforts were rewarded. She won a short-term contract with Fox, and she lined up with the rest of the girls in *Let's Go Places* (1930) even though she was in fact under-age for employment. Later she became briefly a Goldwyn girl in *Whoopee* (1931), and a chorine in Mary Pickford's *Kiki* (1931). A number of walk-on and bit parts followed, including an appearance in Fox's *Cavalcade* (1933).

The succession of small parts she played in film and on stage during 1933–34 brought her invaluable experience. By 1934 she had worked in no less than 15 feature films, and a number of two-reelers with her identity hidden under the name of Frances Dean, in order to avoid legal trouble with RKO studios, who had put her under a five-year contract in 1933 but were unable to find enough work to keep her occupied. Her experience by now covered straight acting in comedy, dancing and (even though she did not have much of a voice) some work as a singer, appearing in live shows as well as in films. In 1936 she appeared again (sixth-billed) in *Follow the Fleet*, with Astaire and Rogers.

By now she could be regarded as established, often playing the gay college girl. She was 20, and getting good photo-coverage in the fan magazines. She climbed, in fact, if not the hard way, at least the sound professional route to stardom, based on experience, versatility and technical application. But she still had some way to go. As she said herself, 'I never will be the Garbo type. There's nothing mysterious about me.'

In 1937 her situation took a new turn; she married Chaplin's ex-child star, Jackie Coogan, who was two years older than herself and in process of suing his parents for the alleged millions he had made as a child. They appeared together in *College Swing*, which starred Bob Hope. She was still a college girl in this picture as well as in *Campus Confessions* (1938) and *Million Dollar Legs* (1939). But her vitality, her beautiful legs, and her obvious figure (she

won a 'Most beautiful figure on the screen' award in 1938) were winning through. By now she was earning her $500 a week, but she still had to resort to 'hoofing' on the stage to make real money. She achieved Broadway in 'Dubarry was a Lady', and made the cover of 'Life' in December 1939.

She got her first starring role in *Down Argentine Way* (1940) after ten years' work in the studios and on the stage, as well as prominence in the photo-publicity field. 'If I mess this up, I'll only have myself to blame,' she said. Although she was actually second to Carmen Miranda, this was the film that finally won her stardom, and principally through her shapely legs. It was immediately followed by *Tin Pan Alley* (1940) with Alice Faye, whose illness had led to Betty's lucky break in *Down Argentine Way*. From now on she was to concentrate on musicals.* *Down Argentine Way* had been shot in colour (by Leon Shamroy), and there is no doubt that, like Rita Hayworth, Betty Grable scintillated in colour. After *Moon Over Miami* (with Don Ameche) and *A Yank in the RAF* (with Tyrone Power), she was set for a top career lasting a decade in colour musicals from 1942, starting with *Song of the Islands*, with Victor Mature. She had top billing in *Springtime in the Rockies* (1942, with John Payne, Carmen Miranda, Cesar Romero), and after this other films followed fast:

1943 *Coney Island*, with George Montgomery and Cesar Romero
Sweet Rosie O'Grady, with Robert Young
1944 *Pin-Up Girl*, with John Harvey.
Pin-Up Girl was the film that made her the Army's pin-up, the 'enlisted man's girl'.

Meanwhile, Betty had eloped to Las Vegas in July 1943 and married her second husband, the band leader Harry James. The following year she had her first child, Victoria Elizabeth. 'Having a baby is the thing for glamour girls now,' she said. 'Lana Turner and me, and now Rita Hayworth.' Other interests she shared with her husband besides music were horse-breeding and racing, in which she was to become expert. The marriage endured a full 20 years; they divorced in 1964.

The musicals went on – principally:

1945 *Billy Rose's Diamond*, with Dick Haymes
The Dolly Sisters, with June Haver
1947 *The Shocking Miss Pilgrim*, with Dick Haymes
Mother Wore Tights, with Dan Dailey
1948 *When My Baby Smiles at Me*, with Dan Dailey
1950 *Wabash Avenue*, with Victor Mature
My Blue Heaven, with Dan Dailey
1951 *Call Me Mister*, directed by Lloyd Bacon and choreographed by Busby Berkeley
Meet Me After the Show, with MacDonald Carey

After this, in effect, Betty went on strike. She was in her middle thirties, and she wanted a change. Marilyn Monroe was the new sex-interest, and later, in 1953, Betty returned to play good-naturedly alongside the new star in

*She tried a straight dramatic role opposite Victor Mature in *I Wake Up Screaming* (*Hot Spot*) in 1941 with little success. She also failed to impress in Ernst Lubitsch's *That Lady in Ermine* (1948) and in Preston Sturges's satiric film, *The Beautiful Blonde from Bashful Bend* (1949).

Above Betty Grable in *College Swing* (1938).

Right In *Three for the Show* (1955). At bottom right, Jack Lemmon can be seen in an early screen appearance.

Below right Betty Grable and Cesar Romero in *Springtime in the Rockies* (1942).

Below Grable again with Cesar Romero in *Coney Island* (1943).

How to Marry a Millionaire, which also featured Lauren Bacall. This was to be the last outstanding film she did. She turned now to live performance in night-clubs and to television, and in 1965 she had a great success on the stage in 'Hello, Dolly'. She had taken to living in Las Vegas during the 1950s, where she enjoyed gambling – 'I love to shoot dice' – and where she owned a ranch-home valued at $100,000.

The nature of Betty Grable's star appeal is her obvious, brassy American vitality; her voluptuousness is clean and efficient as a whistle, and her talk is rough. She knows her own limitations and is blunt about them in her interviews, 'I'm strictly a song-and-dance girl.

I can act enough to get by,' she has said. Her mother once observed, 'She's like any average American girl who makes a million a year.' She also maintained (without any pretentiousness) that she was the Army man's 'inspiration' during the war, the 'enlisted man's girl'. 'A lot of these kids don't have any woman in their lives to fight for,' she added. As a performer, she was tough and likeable, making little attempt at characterization. The parts she played were very close in nature to the qualities she possessed as the leading showgirl of her time, the late 1940s.

She died in July 1973 at Santa Monica, after being ill with lung cancer for over a year.

Betty Grable with Charlotte Greenwood and Carole Landis in *Moon Over Miami* (1941) — three girls and one millionaire.

Betty Grable in *Wabash Avenue* (1950).

Rita Hayworth

Born in New York in 1918, Margarita Carmen Cansino had been trained as a dancer almost from infancy, and on the stage from the age of six. She worked in films as dancer and actress from 1935 before her final, hard-won emergence as a star in 1941 in *Affectionately Yours* and *Blood and Sand*. Her émigré father, Eduardo Cansino, was Spanish, a professional dancer belonging to a celebrated family of dancers in Spain, while her uncle was a distinguished Castilian poet, Rafael Cansinos Assens. Her mother, formerly Volga Haworth, a Ziegfeld girl, was Irish-American, and her aunt was the mother of Ginger Rogers who, seven years older than Margarita, had been a star from the mid-1930s. So Rita Hayworth grew up in the world of show business, touring with her parents. The family finally moved to Los Angeles in 1927, and Margarita was teamed professionally with her father, appearing eventually at the Hotel Caliente where it was easy for them to be seen by film executives. She got her first film contract (a year with Fox) in 1935, using the name Rita Cansino.

She was to appear as dancer and actress (the latter was her real ambition) in a long series of inferior films from Fox's *Charlie Chan in Egypt* and *Dante's Inferno* to Columbia's *Blondie on a Budget* (1940). Her name was changed to Rita Hayworth (the surname adapted from her mother's maiden name of Haworth) when she was signed with Columbia in 1937 at $250 weekly rising to $1,750 over a span of seven years; she was already married to a businessman, Edward Judson, who was much older than herself, and who negotiated this contract for her, since she was still under 20. At the same time she changed the colour of her hair, which was naturally dark, to red. Meanwhile her films continued to be indifferent except that she had two successful supporting parts under distinguished directors in Howard Hawks's *Only Angels Have Wings* (1939), playing to sensational effect opposite Richard Barthelmess, and in George Cukor's *Susan and God* (1940). Then came in 1941 Lloyd Bacon's *Affectionately Yours*, Raoul Walsh's *The Strawberry Blonde* and above all, Mamoulian's *Blood and Sand*, with Tyrone Power and Anthony Quinn as matadors. In *Blood and Sand* she played a society woman with a weakness for matadors; the film was in colour, and her blood-red lips and scarlet fingernails, contrasting with the cool colours of her Spanish mansion – coloration taken from Velasquez – showed her off to glittering advantage. In her final betrayal scene she is clothed sensationally in a crimson evening gown. The legendary Rita Hayworth, another soldier's pin-up, was born in a flood of colour, and she was being paid five times her normal salary.

Then, for the period 1941–44, she specialized in top-class musicals, *You'll Never Get Rich* (with Fred Astaire), *My Gal Sal* (with Victor Mature), *You Were Never Lovelier* (again with Astaire), culminating in *Cover Girl*, directed by Charles Vidor, with Gene Kelly, a musical which bridged the old style and the new, typified by the Kelly-Donen partnership, the musical always on the move, pacing the streets, and using Rita in the image the soldiers liked, the model-cum-showgirl. She could dance, of course, but she could not sing, and her vocals were normally dubbed by Nan Wynn. She is described by John Russell Taylor as, 'long, lanky, a beautiful athletic animal who brought out a new sprightliness, a warmer romantic tone in Astaire'. Like Jean Harlow, she was famous for her tumbling mass of hair, of auburn-gold, crowning her strong features and voluptuous body; she lacked delicacy, and was too voracious to achieve charm easily in her miming of such lyrics as, 'Long Ago and Far Away'.

Another musical, Victor Saville's *Tonight and Every Night* (1945) was followed by Charles Vidor's climactic thriller, *Gilda* (1946) – both were choreographed by Jack Cole – in which she sings, in the night-club sequence, 'Put the blame on Mame, Boys'. Swathed in black satin, and with elbow-length gloves off-setting her magnificent bare arms and shoulders, she entices the men in the audience to reach out their hands to touch her. She was flamboyant sex, and she was to dominate the 1940s as its quintessential, unmistakable sex goddess. *Gilda*, in fact, was to become her facsimile image; as the posters cried, 'There NEVER was a woman like *Gilda*!' Her cameraman said that she had 'flesh that photographs as flesh', and John Kobal has described her special, highly sexed form of dancing, 'Where most dancers move from the legs down, Hayworth dances primarily from the knees up, her shoulders drawn back projecting her body forward in the most enticing manner, only acceptable in the young and very beautiful.' She retained an essentially Latin sensuality.

An aspect of her career which fascinated the press and the public was her celebrated succession of marriages; after the collapse of her marriage with Eddie Judson, her second was to Orson Welles (1943–47)* – by whom she had her daughter, Rebecca – her third to Prince Aly Khan (1949–51) – by whom she had a daughter, Yasmin – her fourth to the singer, Dick Haymes (1953–55), and her fifth to James Hill (1958–61), co-producer of the film, *Separate Tables* (1958). All these marriages resulted in divorce, but for two periods, 1949–51 and 1953–55, she retired from the screen. Orson Welles, however, starred her in his *The Lady From Shanghai*, which appeared after their separation; she plays the predatory wife of a crippled and impotent husband, the lawyer played by Everett Sloane, while Welles plays an itinerant sailor whom she seduces with the intention of framing him for the murder she herself is to commit. She turns from an apparent damsel in distress to a *femme fatale* and

* When she divorced Welles, she made her celebrated remark, 'I just can't take his genius any more.'

Above Rita Hayworth and Fred Astaire in *You Were Never Lovelier* (1942), a Jerome Kern musical.

Above centre Rita Hayworth with Cary Grant in *Only Angels Have Wings* (1939) in which she starred effectively in a flirtatious part playing second lead to Jean Arthur.

Opposite page, top Gilda (1946), with Dick Powell, saw her successful transformation from a musical star to a 'love goddess' in dramatic films.

Opposite page, bottom Rita Hayworth and Fred Astaire in *You'll Never Get Rich* (1941) with music by Cole Porter.

Right Hayworth with Gene Kelly and Phil Silvers in *Cover Girl* (1944), the musical with which she is most closely identified.

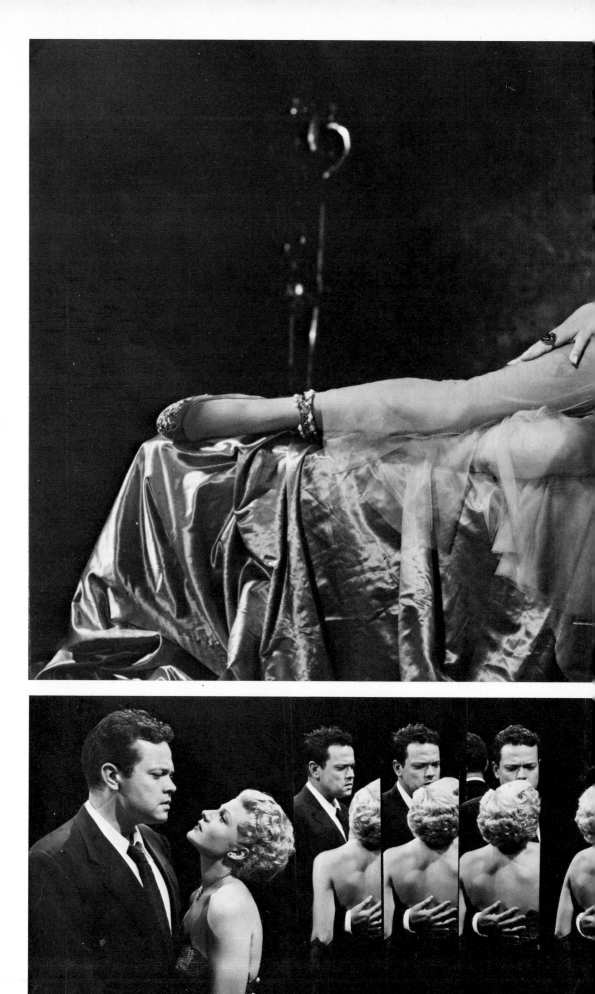

Rita Hayworth in *Salome*
(1953), in a conventional
'love goddess' pose.

With Orson Welles in the
famous mirror-maze climax to
The Lady from Shanghai
(1948).

* The same story, originally
'Rain' by Somerset
Maugham, as that in which
Gloria Swanson had starred
(*Sadie Thompson*, 1928) and
Joan Crawford (*Rain*, 1932).

Below Rita Hayworth and
Rex Harrison in the comedy
The Happy Thieves (1961).

murderess as the film progresses. She does not play for subtlety, rather for symbolic effect. But her marvellous hair was crimped and dyed.

By 1947 she had become one of the top-paid stars in Hollywood, when she worked earning some quarter of a million dollars a year, and at this period she founded her own company to handle her deals with Columbia and other companies. After her marriage with Prince Aly Khan had failed and she decided to return to the screen, her acting was often better than her films, as in *Miss Sadie Thompson* (1953).* When she returned yet again from retirement after her marriage to Dick Haymes, she was to work continuously into the 1970s. She appeared to advantage in George Sidney's musical, *Pal Joey* (1957), and acted effectively in the film version of Rattigan's play, *Separate Tables* (1958). She had matured over the years into a fine actress, which was, after all, her original ambition.

She was later to appear in a number of indifferent films.

THE NINETEEN FIFTIES

Opposite page Typical Bardot tousle-haired, torn-dress, provocative charm. As she appeared in *Viva Maria!* (1965).

Joanne Woodward, one of the more individual actresses in America, with a powerful capacity for characterization in depth.

The 1950s was a decade of post-war disillusion, a period for the sharp questioning of social values, of bitter class and racial challenges, of politically divisive regional wars, and the disintegration of traditional imperial alignments. For films, it was the period which introduced themes of discontent, and the stars, Marilyn Monroe, James Dean, and Marlon Brando, who represented it, came to the fore-front in the United States; directors, too, produced the film of social and psychological malaise, such as Elia Kazan's *A Streetcar Named Desire*, *On the Waterfront*, *East of Eden*, and *Baby Doll*, *Marty*, *Twelve Angry Men*, and other films derived from television plays introduced a new order of realism in acting, and in many cases a reappraisal of the kind of human relationships with which the screen was permitted to deal. It was a period which could produce the raw violences of *The Wild One*, *Rebel without a Cause*, *The Big Knife*, *Riot in Cell Block 11*, and *The Blackboard Jungle*, as well as the sensationalism of *Ace in the Hole*

(corrupt journalism), *Suddenly, Last Summer* (revenge culminating in cannibalism), *The Man with the Golden Arm* (drug addiction), *Paths of Glory*, with its horrifying scenes leading up to the firing-squad, and *The Defiant Ones*, with its racialist confrontations. Yet it was also a period which still maintained the older fashioned idealisms of *High Noon*, or the lightly satiric but romantic humanitarianism of such comedies as *Born Yesterday* and *The Seven Year Itch*. It was a good period for traditionalists such as Ford (*Wagon Master*; *The Sun Shines Bright*; *The Searchers*; *The Horse Soldiers*) and Hitchcock (*Rear Window*; *To Catch a Thief*; *Vertigo*; *North by Northwest*; *Psycho*); but it also saw the rise of a new generation of film-makers concerned with a different and often much harsher approach, among them Stanley Kubrick, Nicholas Ray, Joseph L. Mankiewicz, Stanley Kramer, and Arthur Penn. Several came over from television, including Sidney Lumet, Delbert Mann, John Frankenheimer, and the writers Paddy Chayevsky and Reginald Rose, with their fine ear for colloquial dialogue and feeling for social nuances.

Among the key women stars in America who became fully established during the 1950s were Marilyn Monroe, Elizabeth Taylor, Judy Garland, Jean Simmons, Joanne Woodward, Eva Marie Saint, Debbie Reynolds, Lee Remick, and elsewhere Margaret Leighton, Simone Signoret, Michèle Morgan, Danielle Darrieux, Gina Lollobrigida, and the tempestuous Anna Magnani. The mid-1950s saw the extraordinary response in France to Brigitte Bardot, and the rise of new, more idiosyncratic directors to prominence in Italy – Fellini and Antonioni. Britain, like France, was to find its 'new wave' take full effect only in the 1960s, though in the case of Britain the new wave broke first in the 'live' theatre and in television drama, both during the 1950s.

One sees this decade, therefore, as a period of unease, a bridging time during which the ground was prepared for the more revolutionary 1960s. The nonconformist stars of the period are most typically Marilyn Monroe and Brigitte Bardot – Marilyn Monroe who fought for independence against the old-fashioned image of the sex star, which she seemed both to her vast public and to her producers so pre-eminently to fulfil, and Brigitte Bardot (only eight years younger) who anticipated in Vadim's *Et Dieu créa la Femme* (1955) the fully emancipated adolescent of the future.

Left Jean Simmons as she appeared in *Adam and Evelynne* (1949). One of Britain's most striking young stars, she went to America, where she became eventually an accomplished character actress.

Below Danielle Darrieux, an actress of great spirit and vivacity in the post-war French cinema, as she appeared in *La Ronde* (1950).

Marilyn Monroe

Marilyn Monroe, 'love goddess' supreme of the mid-century, was a creature of unresolved contrasts. Her deep fascination for men and women alike lies in this; indeed, it fascinated herself, for (though modest to the point of inferiority complex) she was insatiably narcissist. But here the division in her begins – narcissist without vanity, she was painfully self-critical, knowing instinctively what was good for her, and yet driven by the insufficiencies in her nature to feel that she too often fell short. Mortified by her unhappy childhood and upbringing ('I was brought up a waif. . . . After all, I have come up from way down') she was determined to be her own mistress, but at the price of making herself dependent to an intolerable degree on dedicated and unremitting service by others. She loved the admiration excited by the splendour of her body – from the wolf whistle of the streets to the acclaim of journalists, critics, photographers, and studio colleagues – yet she abominated the result imposed by the film industry ('A sex symbol becomes a thing. I just hate to be a thing.'). Her lifelong aspiration was to be a 'serious actress', but her nervous excitation in the pursuit of a perfection on the screen satisfactory to her own uncertain judgment ultimately destroyed her capacity to work with all but the rarest and most patient of directors and fellow players. Her demand for love was so intense and complicated that it ravaged all who tried to help her and who spent themselves in ministering to her extravagant and ultimately disordered demands. She was by far the most vulnerable of all those women who achieved lasting stardom on the screen, and this vulnerability was undoubtedly brought about by an instability deep in her nature. This was to a considerable degree a matter of heritage.

She was born Norma Jean Mortensen (though sometimes referred to as Norma Jean Baker, Baker being the father of her elder brother and sister) in Los Angeles on 1 June 1926, the illegitimate daughter of Gladys Monroe, a negative-cutter for MGM. Gladys had been twice married, and her second husband (Mortensen, a Norwegian) had deserted her. Norma's birth, it would seem, was the result of a brief liaison with a fellow film-maker, C. Stanley Gifford, whom Marilyn made shyly abortive attempts to contact later in life. But more significant was the fact that both her grandparents, Della Monroe Grainger and her first husband, Monroe, were committed to State mental institutions, while Norma's mother, Gladys, ended up in a similar condition. They were given to outbursts of violence. Norma Jean's life was actually threatened by her grandmother before her committal. During her childhood she had, on occasion, contact with her mother, and was boarded out before being finally sent for initial schooling to the Los Angeles Orphans Home Society at the age of nine. She also acquired a stutter which (though in some measure controllable) remained with her for life. She was not entirely bereft of affection; in particular, her guardian, Grace McKee (later Goddard) and Grace's aunt, Ana Lower, gave her love, but she was a child with a profound need for parental love, especially that of a father, and a real home.

She was transferred to Emerson Junior High School in 1938, but left school early and married an employee in the Lockheed plant, Jim Dougherty, in June 1942. She was 16, he 22. On the whole, she had been strictly brought up in the Christian Science movement, but by the age of twelve she was precociously mature, and had been dating boys since 1939, at the age of thirteen. She was using make-up, and was aware of her fine figure. When the young couple were eventually separated by war service after two years together, Norma Jean went to work in a war plant where she was discovered by a photographer seeking a model for war worker shots.

Her striking appearance, with its immediate sexual freshness, soon got her on the books of Emmeline Snively's Blue Book Model Agency. This led her into full-time modelling, with a wide-scale use of her pictures, but it broke up her marriage. She was divorced at 19, and ready, as an unmarried girl, to be groomed as a starlet for films. In July 1946 Ben Lyon, who had become casting director for Fox, gave her a contract on sight – $75 a week renewable on a six-month option basis with $25 increases. Her tests in colour proved exceptional, and Ben Lyon renamed her Marilyn Monroe. She wept at what appeared to be her sudden success, but she was to spend the rest of her life living down having been once the fatherless waif and 'orphan', Norma Jean Mortensen and trying to live up to being the wonder-girl, Marilyn Monroe.

But her difficulties, not her opportunities, were beginning. Except for an inborn sense of how to pose for the still camera, she was completely untrained, and her voice (with its stammer) small, shy and undeveloped. The Fox studio already had Betty Grable fully established, and June Haver rising, and Marilyn had to wait four years before she attained very marked success. She was, however, adopted socially by the veteran Fox producer, Joe Schenck, then approaching 70, the first older man to give her the affection and guidance she longed for; they were constantly, and probably innocently, together.

But with bit parts in indifferent films, her career was getting nowhere, though she began training in the Actors Laboratory run by Morris Carnovsky, formerly of the Group Theater in New York. She proved a nervous pupil, unable to concentrate. Zanuck, producer in charge at Fox, refused to renew her contract. Others, however, struck by her air of innocence and helplessness combined with her sexual beauty, moved in; she passed from one agent'

protective grasp to another's, and lived for a while at the YWCA's Studio Club. She went to Columbia for about $125 a week (another six-month option), and fell in love with the studio's middle-aged vocal coach, Fred Karger, who managed to resist her.

Her principal biographer, Fred Lawrence Guiles, is insistent (in spite of her many love-affairs) that she was basically an 'innocent' in such matters, always anticipating marriage where love was concerned. But she had no more luck at Columbia, where Rita Hayworth was the reigning sex queen, than she had had at Fox, and in September 1948, 18 months after her first contract with Fox, she found herself once again unemployed. The following year, during a period of real impoverishment, she posed nude for the photographer, Tom Kelley, and the photographs were to appear anonymously in the notorious 'Golden Dreams' calendar two years later. She received $50 for the session.

Marilyn had come under the influence of Natasha Lytess, a relationship which was to last six years. Trained by Reinhardt in Germany, Natasha had left her country in 1937 and had eventually become a drama coach for Columbia. She took to this lost girl, whose voice was a 'tight squeak' and who seemed utterly unsure of herself even in the minor part she had been given in *Ladies of the Chorus* (1948), singing with the other chorines, 'Everybody needs a Da-Da-Daddy'. Lytess was to become absolute arbiter of Marilyn's performances, working with her on and off the set through every picture until the end of 1954. Dismissed by Columbia, Marilyn made her brief appearance with Groucho Marx in *Love Happy* (1950) – Groucho (detective): What seems to be the problem? Marilyn: Well, men keep following

Below Marilyn Monroe in *The Asphalt Jungle* (1950). Marilyn Monroe played a small part as the mistress of a shady businessman and was widely noticed for the first time.

Below right Complaining to Groucho Marx in *Love Happy* (1948) that men keep following her.

Above Marilyn Monroe
(right) with Dan Dailey in
A Ticket To Tomahawk
(1950), in which she played
a chorus-girl.

Left In *The Fireball* (1950),
a film about roller banked-
track racing, 'America's
newest sports craze', Marilyn
vamped Mickey Rooney
(right).

me all the time – and then she became the adored client of the prominent agent and talent scout, Russian-born Johnny Hyde, who spent thousands of dollars on escorting and promoting her, and even left his wife in order to devote himself to her. He was 53 and she 22, but he taught her something new – sophistication. However, she was not in love with him, and refused his constant offers of marriage, though he was a millionaire.

It was during this association that she got her first important part, that in Huston's film, *The Asphalt Jungle* (1950). Huston proved to be the right director for her, patient and encouraging when she was shaken with nerves. Like Strasberg later, Huston told her nerves were an energy-sign in the sensitive actor's make-up. Hyde also got her the second important part in her career, as the cynical young mistress of George Sanders's sardonic theatre critic in *All About Eve* (1950).

But the producers still seemed against her – Zanuck at Fox, Cohn at Columbia, Schary at MGM. Like the press, they were amused at her aspirations now she was becoming known; to them she was just a breasty blonde. But Hyde, though a sick man with heart trouble, worked on for her and finally won her in 1950 a seven-year contract with Fox which brought her by 1951 up to $750 a week, rising each six months by $250 to $1,500 a week. But she still felt Zanuck thought her a 'sex freak', and this hurt and unnerved her.

In December 1950 Hyde died with Marilyn beside him. She had, however, already been introduced to Arthur Miller in Hollywood, and the first phase of their interest in each other developed. She was already reading widely, erratically, trying to educate herself in art and literature. She was also weight-lifting to develop her breasts. She walked long distances unrecognized in sweat-shirt and jeans for exercise, but avoided a suntan to protect her skin. She ate carefully and drank little. She was interested in the director, Elia Kazan and (through Natasha) the Group Theater, and she was continuing her training now with Michael Chekhov, nephew of the playwright, at his Actors' Studio in Hollywood. Although she was never to become an intellectual, she was moving in the direction of becoming an intelligent nonconformist. The death of Hyde had left her without a man to whom she could turn for guidance. She talked of Miller to Natasha; they corresponded, but he was, it seemed, still securely married. He was not to divorce and marry her until 1956.

During 1951–52 she appeared in a series of indifferent films, such as *As Young as You Feel*, *Love Nest*, *Let's Make it Legal*, and *We're Not Married*. Fritz Lang had trouble with her in *Clash by Night* (for RKO) because she began her chronic habit of being late on the set, and bringing along Natasha to advise and coach her. The press on visits to the studio avoided the top stars (including Paul Douglas, who hated her) and only went in pursuit of 'the girl with the big tits'. She insisted on retakes, and slowed

up production. On the screen, however, she stole the picture, though the studio executives were for a while terrified when a would-be blackmailer revealed she was the naked woman in the recently published 'Golden Dreams' calendar. At the same time she had to face the publicity surrounding the discovery that she had a mother confined in a mental institution, and that she was not, as she and the publicists had maintained, an orphan. *Don't Bother to Knock* (1952), in which she plays a mentally sick girl, was a distressing failure. She was urged, by critics and studio executives alike, to return to sex comedy, and in her insecurity she leaned more than ever on Natasha.

As her box-office value rose phenomenally, Spyros Skouras gave orders that she be nursed,

* In this film she sang with Jane Russell, 'Diamonds are a girl's best friend'. Zanuck validated before a notary that it was genuinely her own voice when the record of the song was issued.

Left With Gregory Ratoff, Anne Baxter, Gary Merrill, George Sanders, and Celeste Holm in *All About Eve* (1950), Marilyn had another small but telling part.

Below Don't Bother to Knock (1952) gave Marilyn the part of a mentally sick baby-sitter.

however difficult she proved to be. She was now being grossly underpaid, since between 1952 and 1953 she starred in Henry Hathaway's *Niagara*, Howard Hawks's musical *Gentlemen prefer Blondes*,* and Jean Negulesco's *How to Marry a Millionaire*. Surprisingly, she was on friendly terms with the 'rival' actresses in these films, Betty Grable, Lauren Bacall, and especially Jane Russell. They sensed her very real fear of acting and joined the great studio conspiracy to protect her, but she outshone everyone in her luminous achievement as a comedienne, at once ingenuous and extrovert in her expression of sexual delight. But when the studio announced her as co-starring with Sinatra in *The Girl in Pink Tights* – for which Sinatra was being paid $5,000 a week – she went

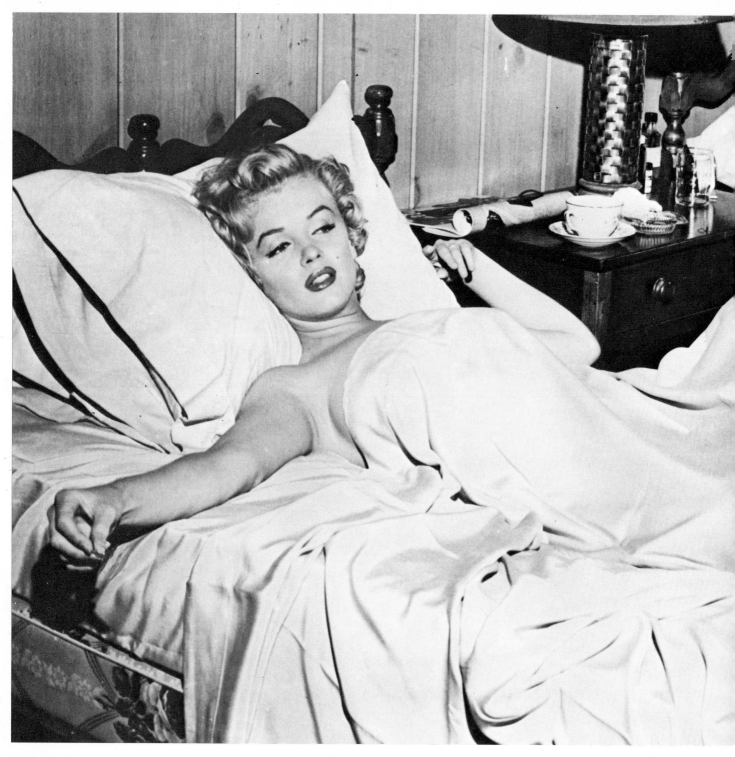

Marilyn had her longest part yet in *Niagara* (1953), in which she displayed her curves against the background of the falls.

on strike and was suspended.

The urge for security finally drove her into a short-lived marriage in January 1954 with Joe DiMaggio, a celebrated baseball-player, who was aged 37 and had retired through injury in 1951, when he had been earning $100,000 a year. Marilyn (aged 27) was earning $1,500 when working, and the studio lifted her suspension as a wedding-present. Like so many star actresses, she yearned to be a 'normal woman', when she was irretrievably abnormal. She set about housework determinedly, including cooking for Joe and his friends. She called him 'Slugger'; his conservatism appealed to her, but he soon proved inhibiting with his addiction to television, to gossiping about sport with his male cronies, and fishing. She was hurt by his shocked disapproval of her skin-tight, revealing clothes and her outrageous response to fan-worship, the ingenuous, open vulgarity of her behaviour in public. She undertook to sing for the American troops in Seoul, but her rendering of 'Do it again' roused such overwhelming response she was asked not to sing it again. Once more, she was surprised and hurt. 'I sing it as a straight, wistful love song,' she said.

After an eight-month absence from the studio, she started her next film in June 1954. This was Walter Lang's *There's No Business like Show Business* (1954), with Donald O'Connor, Dan Dailey and Ethel Merman. Her big solo number was 'Heat Wave', which she insisted should be supervised by her favourite dance director,

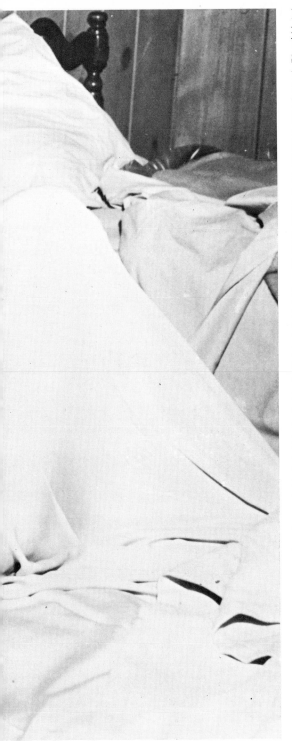

lost time, but suffering from insomnia. She rehearsed her scenes endlessly with Natasha by night, and leaned on her at the studio by day. She insisted on retake after retake. Wilder tolerated her and treated her sympathetically in her part of the 'chick upstairs' who makes Tom Ewell stray from his wife. Meanwhile, Marilyn, in the cultural haven of New York, was conspiring with the star photographer, Milton Greene, to found her own company, Marilyn Monroe Productions, and fight for her rights with Greene as her partner. By October she was seeking divorce from DiMaggio and for a while was too hysterical to work. 'He was indifferent to me as a human being,' she said in court. But she was to remain friends with DiMaggio throughout the rest of her life. It was as a husband she could not tolerate him.

In November *The Seven Year Itch* was finished, and her break with Hollywood followed. By now she was under the influence of Paula and Lee Strasberg as well as Greene. She was in touch, too, with Arthur Miller, whose 15-year marriage was collapsing, though he was not to divorce until June 1956. Her company was set up, and at the end of the year she went into training at Strasberg's Actors' Studio, the celebrated centre in New York for 'Method' acting. Strasberg and his wife were deeply impressed by her potential as an actress, and Marilyn dropped Natasha (her leech-like associate and mentor since *The Asphalt Jungle* in 1949) quite cold, without any form of explanation. This was the least pardonable thing she ever did to a close professional colleague and devoted (if over-attached) helper.

She was now seriously to attempt to build herself into the great actress and integrated person she had always dreamed of becoming. The New York set (Miller, Greene and his wife Amy, the Strasbergs – not by any manner of means all in favour of each other) were to guide her in the achievement of this psychotherapeutic miracle. Kazan (who also favoured her) was associated with Strasberg, but had been temporarily alienated from Miller when they had taken opposite sides during the 1952 hearings of the Un-American Activities Sub-Committee. But Marilyn's instinctive non-conformity (tinged always by her opposite desire to conform, as in her desire for love and marriage) drove her to the 'Left' in New York, though she stayed clear from party politics. As for her private problems (her depression; her rages; her insomnia; her psychologically induced sickness, and so forth) she resorted constantly to psychiatrists, regarding psychoanalysis as complementary to her new approach to training under Strasberg.

For virtually a year, she put aside Marilyn the glamour-star and took to the informal guise of slacks, sweat-shirts, and a face clean of make-up. With Strasberg she attempted (apparently with success) to play Blanche in 'A Streetcar named Desire' and Anna in O'Neill's 'Anna Christie'. Strasberg, who has defined acting in depth as 'the ability to respond to imagined stimuli with the same

Jack Cole, another of her props when her self-confidence collapsed in the face of the hard, efficient professionalism of her co-stars. However, Irving Berlin liked her style in her other solo number, 'After you get what you want, you don't want it.' 'It took Marilyn's interpretation to make me see how sexy it was,' he said. But she was frequently ill during this work, and began to turn to alcohol for relief.

By autumn her separation from Joe was on the way. He was appalled at the notorious skirt-blowing incident staged in September by Billy Wilder for *The Seven Year Itch* while on location in New York. Press photographers were present, and unfavourable comment followed. She had gone straight from one film to the other without a break, catching up with

Right In Joshua Logan's *Bus Stop* (1956), Marilyn was Cherie, who sang songs to rodeo cowboys and yearned for a mink coat.

Opposite page, top Singing with Jane Russell 'When Love Goes Wrong' in *Gentlemen Prefer Blondes* (1953).

Opposite page, centre With Cameron Mitchell, Betty Grable, and Lauren Bacall in *How To Marry A Millionaire* (1953).

Opposite page, bottom In *The Seven Year Itch* (1955) Marilyn plays 'Chopsticks' to an infatuated Tom Ewell.

* A whole new generation of American stage and screen stars sprang from work in the Actors' Studio, including Brando, Rod Steiger, Eli Wallach, Paul Newman, James Dean, Montgomery Clift, Tom Ewell, Kim Stanley, Shelley Winters, Geraldine Page, Julie Harris, Eva Marie Saint.

† In *Let's Make Love* she sang Cole Porter's 'My Heart Belongs to Daddy'. In *Some Like It Hot* she sang the numbers, 'Running Wild', 'I wanna be loved by You', 'Sweet Sue', and 'I'm thru' with love'.

intensity as one does to real stimuli', said of her, 'I saw that what she looked was not what she really was, and what was going on inside was not what was going on outside, and that always means there may be something there to work with. In Marilyn's case, the reactions were phenomenal . . . a door opened and you saw a treasure of gold and jewels. It is unusual to find the underlying personality so close to the surface and so anxious to break out.' He held her to be 'as good as Brando'. Her stammer, which stopped entirely in class, Strasberg considered originated from her being forced in childhood to say things which were contrary to what she really thought and felt.*

Marilyn's love-affair with Arthur Miller continued, and they finally married in July 1956. On the back of her wedding picture of herself and Miller she wrote, 'hope, hope, hope'. Marilyn had meanwhile through her company comes to terms again with Fox (where Buddy Adler had replaced Zanuck) and contracted to appear from 1956 in a series of films at $100,000 a film, plus $500 a week expenses; of this she herself was to receive half, Greene (her partner) receiving three-quarters of the rest. The idea was that she should work in two films a year to clear for herself $100,000. She had director as well as subject approval, and the directors she approved included Cukor, Huston, Wilder, and Joshua Logan. She returned to Hollywood, after over a year's absence, arriving in the grand manner, received by swarms of reporters.

Logan was to direct her in *Bus Stop*, with Paula Strasberg replacing Natasha as side-line observer-adviser. Logan thought very highly of Marilyn – 'as near a genius as any actress I ever knew. . . . She has the unfashionable mysteriousness of a Garbo. . . . Monroe is pure cinema. How rarely she has to use words. How much she does with her eyes, her lips, with slight, almost accidental gestures.' (Wilder was to agree, saying, 'There has never been a woman with such voltage on the screen with the exception of Garbo.') In *Bus Stop* Marilyn played Cherie, a barely literate entertainer with designs on Hollywood; she played her like a real person, Method-style, and Logan encouraged her to improvise while he kept the cameras turning. She sang, 'That old black magic' in stockings covered with darns. She was so anxious to succeed she was often in a paroxysm of nervous hysteria before going on the set.

She had made *Bus Stop* prior to her marriage with Miller. Immediately afterwards, the couple left for London where she was to film *The Prince and the Showgirl* (an adaptation of Rattigan's play, 'The Sleeping Prince') with Laurence Olivier, who was also to direct. This was a production sponsored by her own company, which had acquired the film rights in Rattigan's play. Olivier had produced 'The Sleeping Prince' on the stage with Vivien Leigh as the showgirl. Though the film was to turn out more than adequate, the association with Olivier, on which she had pinned high hopes, proved to be disastrous. He could not tolerate her utter lack of self-discipline; he called her a 'professional

amateur', and the tension between them (born of her constant lateness and absences, her chronic inability to take direction from him, and her nervous seizures in spite of his assumed patience with her) led Miller to understand to the full that his role in this marriage was to be her guardian, protector, go-between with exasperated colleagues, and the sounding-board for her distraught rages, tears and hysteria. It has to be remembered on her behalf that she suffered from intense menstrual pains, and although she desired to have children, suffered a miscarriage in 1958, and was forced to have two pregnancies terminated, in 1957 and again in 1962, shortly before her death. In 1957 she took legal action to break up her partnership with Greene, and Miller found himself left alone with his charge.

But Miller, like some others, loved her deeply, and the marriage (considered by many as an extraordinary match) was, in the circumstances of Marilyn's ambitions, natural talent and intelligence, potentially a sound one. Miller was an artist first and an 'intellectual' second, an active man with a Leftist outlook, not a recluse. He appreciated Marilyn's natural wit, her talent for making intuitively accurate judgments, her fight against Hollywood and her nonconformism, her avid, but disorganized, reading of literature, poetry and philosophy. She was, perhaps, in some awe of his intellect and his high position among the New York intelligentsia as Pulitzer prize-winner for 'Death of a Salesman'. But for the period of the marriage (July 1956 to their final break following work on *The Misfits* in November 1960 and divorce in 1961), Miller, driven near distraction in his efforts to look after his wife, had produced next to nothing as a writer apart from *The Misfits*, the screenplay he wrote for her, published initially as a story in 1957.

Marilyn had a stormy passage with her next film, *Some Like It Hot*, in which her company had shares. It was made by Wilder in less sympathetic mood with Marilyn, who played the singer, Sugar Kane, and, mindful of her appearance, had wanted colour. (The film could not be in colour in case the men dressed as women – Jack Lemon and Tony Curtis – wearing coloured make-up on the screen would invite censorship reprisals.) So Marilyn started work in a bad mood, arriving late from the first day onwards. Tony Curtis could not stand her; 'It's like kissing Hitler,' he said. The film ran far over budget, costing some $3 million, but by 1962 it had grossed $14 million, and earned Marilyn herself some $3 million. But by then she was dead.

Her next film, *Let's Make Love* (1960) led to her meeting with the French actor and singer, Yves Montand, whose personality intrigued Marilyn so much that she fell obsessively in love while Miller was away in New York. The press discovered this and went into the attack. Cukor, her director on this film, looking back after 15 years said to Gavin Lambert, 'Truth to tell, I think she was quite mad. . . . Every day was an agony of struggle for her.' However, he admits, 'She had this absolute, unerring touch with comedy. . . . She acted as if she didn't quite understand why it was funny, which is what made it so funny.'† Her ordinary voice was quite unattractive, he said, 'so she invented this appealing baby voice'. She kept her mouth open; when it was closed her face changed, strengthened, looked determined. 'The face wasn't all that pretty, but it moved in a wonderful way, it was a wonderful movie face.' Cukor felt she was a mass of contradictions, sweetness and toughness, shrewdness and helplessness, gentleness and violence, modesty and exhibitionism. He was dead against the influence on her of the Method-style of part-studying. On the set she would constantly break down, fluff her lines, unable to sustain a shot right through. 'You had to shoot piecemeal,' said Cukor, 'but curiously enough, when you strung everything together, it was complete. . . . There was an excitement about her.'

The Misfits temporarily reunited Marilyn and her husband during the shooting on location in Nevada through the summer of 1960. As a result, it was among the most painful of all her productions. It was reputedly the most expensive black and white picture ever made.

Right With Jack Lemmon in *Some Like It Hot* (1959), Marilyn Monroe's most successful film.

Below right With Laurence Olivier and Sybil Thorndyke in *The Prince and the Showgirl* (1957), a much-publicized but unsuccessful film. Monroe and Olivier were unhappy working together.

* There have been more biographical and other published studies of Marilyn Monroe than of any other film actress. The most reliable so far is that by Fred Lawrence Guiles, 'Norma Jean: the Story of Marilyn Monroe' (1969), but it should be supplemented by the interviews and quotations in Maurice Zolotow's 'Marilyn Monroe' (1961). The most striking collection of photographs are those in 'Marilyn Monroe' (1974) compiled by John Kobal, with an excellent essay by David Robinson, and in Norman Mailer's book, mentioned below. In 1964 Arthur Miller's play, 'After the Fall', directed by Elia Kazan for the Lincoln Center in New York, purged the trauma of his marriage to her through thinly veiled fictional characters; it was written, he said, 'with respect for her agony – but with love', but he was severely criticized. So, too, was Norman Mailer when in 1973 in a biographical study called 'Marilyn' he claimed her death could well have been political murder and that the married man with whom she was associating in 1962 was Robert Kennedy, the Attorney-General. Sympathetic studies of her by women include a profile in 'Life' by Clara Booth Luce and Joan Mellen's recent short biography, 'Marilyn Monroe' (1973), which contains a substantial bibliography.

Even Huston's humanity and patience as director were strained, and the open alienation between Miller and Marilyn led to unendurable complications and disputes. Yet she was happy to be linked with Clark Gable, the idol of her youthful cinema-going, and with Montgomery Clift, who matched her in the personal distress he had to endure. She plays the sexually promiscuous woman seeking a divorce in Reno, and at the same time falling in love with the men she finds there – most of all with the elderly, primitive but still virile Clark Gable. The heat on location was intense, and Marilyn's difficulties and outright illness in August delayed the production which should have finished by mid-September but lasted in all 90 days until 4 November, the last two weeks being back in Hollywood. Gable, already a sick man and overstrained by the heat and the prolonged commitment, died of a heart attack less than two weeks later, on 16 November.

Apart from the brief, abortive work with Cukor on *Something's Got to Give* in April 1962, this was to be the end of Marilyn's career. She was unfit for work, fighting insomnia and acute depression and violent hysteria with near-lethal doses of Nembutal, which rendered her incapable of standing upright the following morning. She had obtained the drug surreptitiously and it only increased her depression. She looked terrible. In August 1961 she returned to Los Angeles for further treatment and psychiatric examination. She was withdrawn from Nembutal and given less harmful drugs.

Nevertheless, during 1961 she became increasingly dependent on drugs. Her constant companion and guardian now was her press secretary, Pat Newcomb. She seemed to be securing a new hold on life towards the end of the year, and she even set up a new establishment in Hollywood the following February.

But work on *Something's Got to Give* had to be abandoned in the spring. She deserted the picture, and was suspended. She flew to New York, however, and sang 'Happy Birthday' in Madison Square Gardens on the night of President Kennedy's birthday. She was a close friend of Peter Lawford and his wife, Pat, the sister of the President and of Robert Kennedy, the Attorney-General. Then she returned to Hollywood and consented for the second time in her life to be photographed nude by a group of top photographers for press and magazine publication.

She was 36, and she had formed another attachment with an unnamed married man in high place in the East. This was kept strictly secret, but DiMaggio, her open escort, and a few others knew of it. On 20 July a pregnancy had to be terminated, and she returned four days later to her depression and her drugs. On the night of Saturday, 4 August, she was found dead in her bedroom; she had taken an overdose of Nembutal, and her outstretched hand rested on her bedside telephone. Her death was recorded as 'probable suicide', but those few closest to her were to maintain it was a terrible accident and that she died while attempting to esperately and unsuccessfully raise help by ringing the numbers of her friends.

There was no next of kin to care for her body. The autopsy revealed there was poison (unspecified by the police) in her stomach as well as Nembutal and chloral hydrate in her system, with the presence of burns in the mouth and digestive tract. The telephone company's record of her outgoing calls was also impounded, probably because one of them was to the man in high place whose name had to be protected.*

Shortly before her death, Marilyn had been interviewed at her home for 'Life' magazine by its Associate Editor, Richard Meryman, on whom she had made a favourable impression, except that he felt 'the house was saturated with paranoia'. He is quoted as saying that, 'he had never met a more delightful person, nor one who would be more impossible to live with.' In the 'Life' interview, the best expression of her philosophy as woman and star, she said many forthright and revealing things; some have already been quoted. She hated, she said, to be ridiculed: 'Please don't make me a joke. . . . I want to be an artist, an actress with integrity. My work is the only ground I've ever had to stand on. I seem to have a whole superstructure with no foundation – but I'm working on the foundation.' And she added: 'I want to say that the people – if I am a star – the people made me a star – no studio, no person, but the people did. . . . I'm one of the world's most self-conscious people. I really have to struggle. . . . Creativity has got to start with humanity, and when you're a human being, you feel, you suffer. . . . There's a need for aloneness which I don't think most people realize for an actor. It's almost having certain kinds of secrets for yourself that you'll let the whole world in on only for a moment, when you're acting.' But, she said, 'If I'm going to be a symbol of something I'd rather have it sex than some other things they've got symbols of!'

Marilyn Monroe and Clark Gable in *The Misfits* (1961), the last completed film for either star.

Ingrid Bergman

Ingrid Bergman, who was born in Stockholm on 29 August 1915, daughter of an artist, lost her mother at the age of two, her father at the age of 12, and the aunt who was then caring for her six months later. An uncle succeeded as guardian. 'I became extremely shy and withdrew into a dream world of my own imagination,' she has said of this period. As a schoolgirl, she felt herself tall, ungainly and self-conscious. But she was determined to become an actress, because through acting her inhibitions could be set aside. In spite of opposition from her uncle, she succeeded in 1933 at the age of 18 in entering the Royal Dramatic Theatre School, where Garbo had studied a decade earlier and where Ingmar Bergman's great actor, Gunnar Björnstrand was her contemporary. At the same time, she let herself come under the firm guidance of a young dentist, Peter Aron Lindstrom, who was almost ten years older than herself. She was later to marry him in 1937, and give birth to her first daughter, Friedel Pia, in 1938.

Still shy, but the picture of health and vitality, she attracted notice during 1933–34 as a result of the leading parts she undertook virtually from the start in Swedish films, and from 1935 she worked in a number of Gustav Molander's productions, playing parts of increasing demand, and appearing opposite Lars Hanson, Victor Sjöström (Seastrom), Gosta Ekman, and other leading players of the Swedish cinema, while in 1938 she appeared in a German UFA film directed by Carl Froelich; she spoke German fluently. In these films, which belong to her early twenties, she played always the woman in love, but faced with difficulties, in one bearing the illegitimate child of a pastor, in another being in love with a married man, in yet another involved in justifiable homicide, and so forth. She played in the Swedish version of *A Woman's Face*, the melodrama in which Joan Crawford was to star in 1941. She played women who combined great sincerity with a powerful erotic impulse, and her marked beauty and charm were fully developed early in her career.

The Swedish film that took her to Hollywood was *Intermezzo* (1936), in which she had played a young and brilliant student of music infatuated with a celebrated violinist and taking him from his wife. Selznick instructed his story editor, Katharine Brown, to secure the remake rights and to go to Sweden and 'not come home without a contract with Miss Bergman'. He wanted to put her under a seven-year contract, but only persuaded the Lindstroms to venture on a single, trial production in Hollywood – the American version of *Intermezzo* (1939; director Gregory Ratoff), in which she played opposite Leslie Howard. In this her success was instantaneous. Compared with most Hollywood actresses she appeared unmannered an natural, vivacious and sincere, with a warm an unforced charm which was irresistible. Sh was, however, worried about her heavy Swedis accent; Selznick put her mind at rest by sayin he would dub her lines which 'read badly'. H was more concerned about her photography 'Unlike almost any player of importance I know of, the difference in her photography is th difference between great beauty and complet lack of beauty,' he wrote to Harry Stradling who was later replaced as director of photo graphy for *Intermezzo* by Gregg Toland. Selznic again issued detailed instructions to Tolan how she should be photographed, avoiding th 'bad side of her face' or making her appear to big, paying attention to the make-up of he mouth, and her hair-style. He insisted her ey brows remain unplucked, setting a new fashio for eyebrows *au naturel*. It was essential to he looks that she appeared to be without make-up He realized that her beauty and her emotiona impact combined to create a mature and alto gether new screen personality which heralde the naturalistic acting of the 1940s. She was a once sensitive and intelligent, and wholesomel sensual.

Looking back at his first meeting with her Selznick has said, 'The minute I looked at her I knew I had something. She had an extra ordinary quality of purity and nobility and definite star personality that is very rare.' H was charmed by her conscientiousness and con sideration for others; she virtually lived on th set and was prepared to work all hours; her feel ing for her work and for everyone else's wa one of complete dedication.

It was the onset of the war, however, rathe than the furtherance of her career whic finally decided the Lindstroms to move t America. Here she had to wait for a film whil under contract to Selznick, and received hi permission to star on Broadway in 'Liliom with Burgess Meredith (March 1940). B September she was back in Hollywood, and th long roster of American films belonging to th period 1941–49 began.

In 1941 she gave sympathetic performance in the lesser kind of films, *Adam had Four Son* and *Rage in Heaven* (both featuring unhapp love-affairs), but in Victor Fleming's *Dr Jekyl and Mr Hyde* (1941) she was permitted to tak on the bad woman for a change, the barmai who practises seduction only to become Hyde' victim, and she managed to steal the picture But it was Michael Curtiz's *Casablanca* (1942 that assured her a place in Hollywood's esteem Here she was matched as the leading woma with a whole range of established stars, in cluding Claude Rains, Humphrey Bogart, Pete Lorre, Conrad Veidt, and Sydney Greenstreet The film, though essentially melodrama, wa one of the best non-documentary-style feature to be made in America during the war years. S successful was she that she was asked to tak over the key part of Maria in *For Whom the Bel Tolls* (1943; director Sam Wood). She achieve an Academy Award nomination. James Age

Opposite page Ingrid Bergman in 1947, when she was making films in Hollywood and was one of the top box-office attractions.

Right In *Dr Jekyll and Mr Hyde* (1941), Ingrid Bergman changed parts with Lana Turner, and played a good-time girl.

Below *Casablanca* (1942) made Bergman a star when she performed perfectly as Humphrey Bogart's lover.

wrote of her performance: 'She really knows how to act, in a blend of poetic grace with quiet realism which almost never appears in American pictures.' For the remake of *Gaslight* (1944; director George Cukor) she won her first Academy Award.

What she stood for was sincerity, a direct emotional involvement in these fictional characters which led the movement towards far more actual, naturalistic women in star roles on the screen. She even brought credibility to the over-sentimental *The Bells of Saint Mary's* (1945), and then found herself playing a psychiatrist in Hitchcock's *Spellbound* (1945) with Gregory Peck. This was followed by *Notorious* (1946), in which she becomes involved in spying through a love-affair, the innocent involved through

weakness (love and alcoholism) in wrong-doing.* *Arch of Triumph*, in which she appeared 'out of image' as a prostitute, was unsuccessful and *Joan of Arc* (a character she had always wanted to play), made after her outstanding success on Broadway in Maxwell Anderson's play, 'Joan of Lorraine' in 1946, was equally disastrous at the box-office. Hitchcock's *Under Capricorn*, made in Britain – in which she was yet another alcoholic – was one of Hitchcock's least successful productions.

Her cataclysmic relationship with the Italian director, Roberto Rossellini developed in 1949, shattering her reputation in the eyes of her American public, especially the women's clubs. Her marriage with the over-rigid Lindstrom had already begun to suffer the strains of her

Right Bergman as a nun with Bing Crosby as a priest in RKO's sentimental *The Bells of St Mary's* (1945).

Below Anastasia (1957) was the film for which Bergman returned to Hollywood and won her second Oscar.

Left Bergman in *Stromboli* (1950), her first film with Roberto Rossellini.

Below With Cary Grant in *Notorious* (1946), the last of a run of hits which ended when Bergman's private life began to get adverse publicity.

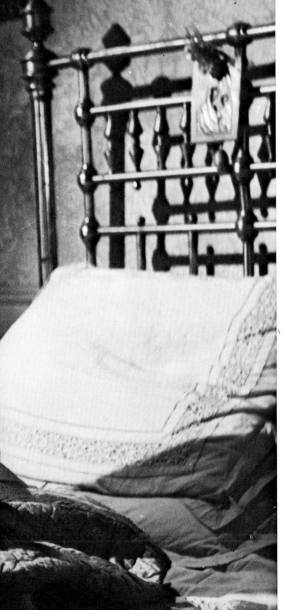

Bergman and Anthony Quinn in *The Visit* (1964), which proved a failure.

life in Hollywood. She enjoyed the social round; he did not. There were many press-inspired rumours of her propensity for infatuation – now with this actor, now with that. She asked for a divorce during 1947; she was unhappy, 'I was exploding inside,' she said. After seeing Rossellini's film *Paisa* in 1948, she had written him the 'Ti amo' letter (her only words in Italian) in which she proposed they work together. She received an enthusiastic cable back, and met Rossellini while she was making *Under Capricorn.*

Stromboli, financed by Howard Hughes at RKO, went into production in March 1949. She was still working in association with her husband, but her feeling for Rossellini became so strong that the rumours of their love filled the press. The film, part Italian in feeling and part Hollywood in the final cutting, proved a further disaster in 1950, the year she gave birth to Robertino, her son by Rossellini. The scandal of the child's illegitimacy delighted the press, and the furore was one of the most shocking in the history of relations between the press, the public and the stars of the cinema. As she said herself, 'People didn't expect me to have emotions like other women.' Only after the birth of Rossellini's child did she finally file a suit for divorce from Lindstrom. The public image so carefully built up by Selznick 'backfired', as he said. Her Mexican proxy marriage to Rossellini followed in May 1950, followed by Lindstrom's suit for divorce which he obtained, with exclusive guardianship of their daughter. In 1952 she had two more children, giving birth

to twin daughters, Isabella and Isotta.

During the period 1950–55, she appeared in a series of films directed by Rossellini – in addition to *Stromboli*, there were, *Europa 51, We the Women, Journey into Italy, Joan at the Stake* (based on the play by Claudel, and on the opera-oratorio he created with the composer, Honneger, in which Joan has a speaking part only), and *Fear* (made in Germany). The tensions arising from the continued lack of success with these films, and especially with their tour of the stage version of 'Joan at the Stake', led to the dissolution of their relationship. She insisted at the nadir of her career on working with other directors, including Renoir (*Elena et les Hommes*, 1951), and on appearing in 'Tea and Sympathy' on the Paris stage. Rossellini left for India and other *amours*, and she was left free.

Renoir, who had great faith in her and wanted to put her on the screen in a cheerful role, unfortunately did not manage to restore her image. She had to await her forgiveness in America for this. The gesture came at last in 1956, with an offer worth $200,000. She was reintroduced to the international public by 20th Century-Fox in *Anastasia* (1957; director Anatole Litvak) with Yul Brynner. It won her her second Academy Award. At the same time Rossellini returned from India with the wife of an Indian director; divorce followed, and in December 1958 Ingrid married Lars Schmidt, a Swedish-born impresario. She lives in Sweden and in Paris, and pursues a career shared out between films, television, and the stage.

The more celebrated films of her later period in addition to *Anastasia* have been the comedy *Indiscreet* (1958; director Stanley Donen), *The Inn of the Sixth Happiness* (1958; director, Mark Robson), and *Goodbye Again* (1961; director Anatole Litvak, a film based on Françoise Sagan's 'Aimez-vous Brahms?'). In the last she played a woman in middle life who fears the loss of love. In 1964 she did a short film in Sweden – a story called 'The Necklace' from Maupassant, part of the episodic *Simultantia*, directed by Gustav Molander and co-starring with Gunnar Björnstrand. She has also starred in *Cactus Flower* (1969) with Goldie Hawn and Walter Matthau and in *A Walk in Spring Rain* (1970), with Anthony Quinn, these adding little to her reputation, though the first was a commercial success. Increasingly she has turned to the stage and television to fulfil her undaunted acting ambitions, appearing with success, for example, in 'Hedda Gabler', 'A Month in the Country' and Maugham's 'The Constant Wife'.

Bergman received good notices for *Cactus Flower* (1969), in which she appeared with Walter Matthau, and which was a big success.

Brigitte Bardot

Brigitte Bardot had the most desirable kind of middle-class upbringing – she was the daughter of a Parisian industrialist and she had a smart, highly cultured mother. She was born on 28 September 1934, and lived as a child in a fashionable area of Paris. She attended a private school, and from the age of six was also given regular instruction in ballet, which was one of her mother's principal interests. She emerged in post-war France of the 1950s a mature-looking, beautifully shaped 17-year-old girl, a natural model for the photographers and an immediate success.

She worked originally as a fashion model, fashion being another of her mother's obsessions. She achieved the cover of 'Elle' in May 1950 and was tested at the age of 15 by Marc Allégret for a film which did not reach production. The tests, however, encouraged her to study dramatic art, urged on by Allégret's young assistant, Roger Vadim Plemmianikov, the future Roger Vadim, who got her small parts in unimportant films, in one of which *La Fille sans Voiles*, she appeared momentarily naked. The future Roger Vadim, a stage actor who had also been a journalist, urged her to marry him while she was still a minor, and when her parents refused consent she made a serious attempt at suicide. They were married with conventional ceremony on 20 December 1952. He was 24 and she 18.

Vadim was determined to succeed, and he had a gift for self-promotion. He also knew how to exploit the charms of his young wife to achieve their fortunes. He knew the world of the popular press well, just as he knew the world of the commercial cinema, having worked with Allégret since 1947. He changed Brigitte's image and way of life from that of the young society beauty he had married to that of a rebellious and challenging teenager of the 1950s. To earn money she appeared in small parts in many films including René Clair's *Les Grands Manœuvres*. In 1954 she was in Robert Wise's *Helen of Troy* in Italy, and the following year she was a French 'sex-kitten' in the British film, *Doctor at Sea*. She played Poppaea in the Italian film, *Nero's Weekend*, and in 1956 starred for the first time as a dancer in *Cette Sacrée Gamine*, which Vadim scripted.

The image soon to be launched on the world by Vadim was maturing – the sulky pout, the casual sexuality, the provocative gaiety in confrontation with men. Her contract value rose from 2.5 to 15 million old francs. In other films she did strip-tease, and in *La Lumière d'en face* she openly stripped and bathed naked. Vadim wanted to make her, as he put it, 'the unrealizable dream of all married men'.

So the time had come for the film which was to give her a world reputation, Vadim's first film as director, *Et Dieu créa la Femme* (1956).

She was 23. The film (in colour) was financed by Raoul Lévy on the strength of the collaboration of Curt Jurgens; Bardot was to play Juliette, an orphan girl of 18 in Saint-Tropez involved with three men. Bardot danced a provocative mambo, and gave everything to the semi-nude love scenes which set even the French censor problems. Timed exactly right, the film became a youth-and-sex manifesto not merely in France but in the United States, where its fame was enhanced by the scandal it caused. Fulminations were launched by those opposed to the film's open advocacy for women's freedom of choice in sexual partners. The film grossed ten times its cost in the United States alone, $4 million in two years. Bardot stood for the life of immediate, spontaneous pleasure, without moral inhibition ('the future was invented to spoil the present'); she was as aggresively irresponsible as she was shamelessly female. She had the lithe, undeniably sexual appetite of a graceful young animal. She broke the rules as much through innocence as conscious nonconformity, and utter rejection of the sheltered, middle-class values in which she, and many in her audience, had been raised.

On the whole Bardot, or BB as she came to be called, has appeared in few films of distinction in their own right. Vadim repeated her new image in *Les Bijoutiers du Clair de Lune*, shot in Spain with Stephen Boyd. Among the films of the period the most notable was Claude Autant-Lara's *En cas de Malheur* (1958; English title, *Love is my Profession*), with Jean Gabin and Edwige Feuillère, in which she plays an amoral 20-year-old who seduces the distinguished lawyer who defends her on a robbery charge, a stormy affair which ends with his death. In her frank demand for sexual pleasure she is without any feminine guile, and the film contrasts her 'honesty', for what it is worth, with the sophisticated behaviour of the 'woman of the world' played by Edwige Feuillère. Gabin and Feuillère, dubious at first of appearing with her, claimed afterwards to have found her charming and intelligent, but at the same time nervous, full of self-doubt, and uncertain both of her talent and her beauty.

Meanwhile, her private life had hit the headlines. As early as the summer of 1956 her love-affair with her leading man in *Et Dieu créa la Femme*, Jean-Louis Trintignant, had reached the French press, and led to a friendly separation from Vadim after barely four years of marriage. Bardot's star value rose in consequence to 30 million old francs a picture. BB was exercising the very freedom which her films portrayed. She was divorced from Vadim in 1957, but she was frequently to work with him again.

In order to avoid censorship and make her allowable viewing to the youth she was supposed to represent, she played a heroine of the French Resistance (and did not once strip) in Christian-Jaque's war film, *Babette s'en va-t-en guerre* (1959); in the same year she married her leading man in this film, 24-year-old Jacques Charrier (son of a retired Army Colonel) on

Bardot in *The Lighthouse Keeper's Daughter* (1952), a minor film made when she was 18.

Alone and distraught, she cuts her veins in her prison cell. Clouzot, a director of the older generation, attempted in this film to contrast the unrelenting morality of the French courts with the new, amoral life of youth; the truth, Clouzot shows, becomes distorted through the legal process. Dominque is the victim not only of her own self-indulgence but of a scheme of values in which she has no place. Clouzot admired Bardot's acting capacity – 'she has a very large range,' he said. 'She can pass with ease from comedy to drama and even to tragedy.'

On 28 September 1960, Bardot took an overdose of barbiturates, slit her wrists with a

18 June. Her love life continued to cause sensational comment. The public alternated their moods of 'Bardolatry' with open affront at the way of life she was described as living. Her marriage was to last only a matter of months, but in January 1960 she gave birth to a son, Nicolas Charrier.

Her situation in many respects became parallel to that of Marilyn Monroe. Both actresses at this time were world 'personalities', 'sex-symbols', and public curiosity about their private lives was at its height. Bardot was 25, and she had already appeared in 24 films. She had even become the centre of attention for the sociologists, who saw her, as one contemporary press profile claims, as 'the symbol of the loneliness and insecurity of modern youth'. She was a new and disturbing myth, and her image had much in common with Nabokov's Lolita, the 'nymphet' or 'baby-doll' turned provocative 'child-woman', or the girls in the novels of the youthful Françoise Sagan. But in 1959, shortly after her marriage, she was summed up in the same press profile as likeable, unpretentious, disinterested in politics or in intellectual pursuits, interested in money but frugal in her way of life, concerned about success and the nature of her popularity, her public image which, now that she was 25, would have to be remodelled in the near future. Meanwhile she had become, as a banner headline in the London 'News Chronicle' put it, 'one of the most astonishing myths of the post-war world'.

But 1960 was to be her year of acute crisis. The birth of her child was followed shortly by the break-up of her marriage when she fell in love with Sami Frey, with whom she was appearing in the most controversial of her films so far, *La Verité*. She was making this under the intense and demanding direction of Henri-Georges Clouzot, and the film was publicized in advance as showing a new Bardot, Bardot the great actress. *La Verité* presents the trial of a young girl who steals her sister's student boyfriend. He quarrels with her over her affairs with other men, and eventually she shoots him. She follows this with an attempt at suicide.

azor-blade like the heroine in the film, and lay own to die in the garden of a villa in Cabrolles, ear Menton. She was discovered in time and ushed to a clinic accompanied by reporters nd press photographers who happened to be here. The whole world was shocked she could ave been driven to this extreme. Like Monroe, he had come to lean for guidance on a small emale coterie (known as the 'Bardot Mafia') vho hedged her in. But the monstrous nature f her fame, the invasion of her privacy by ersistent journalists, the pressures of the film he had just completed, and the troubles in her ove life finally caught up with her. Shortly efore her suicide attempt she had given a press

Above Bardot in the first film she made in Britain: as a 'sex-kitten' with Dirk Bogarde in *Doctor At Sea* (1955).

Left Bardot was the daughter of a night-club owner in the comedy *Cette Sacrée Gamine* (1956).

interview in which she had said, 'I must kill the monster that is in me. I must chase away the intruder who has the name of BB. I want to be able to say, BB is no more. Vive Brigitte!'

The film, *La Vie Privée* (*A Very Private Affair*, with Marcello Mastroianni), was the work to which she turned in 1961. Directed by Louis Malle, *La Vie Privée* was based on her own life; it is the study of the situation of a film star whose real life is destroyed by the legend her screen self has created, as a result of which she is mobbed by fans and pursued by the press. She loses the man she really loves, and the film ends with her stylized death, what Malle called, 'an end for a mythological heroine'.

She had already severed her connection with her original producer, Raoul Lévy, once her contract had expired. She wanted to establish her independence. She worked with Vadim and another director, Michel Boisrond on films of no great importance. She appeared to be settling down with a 'mature' version of her inescapable self, that part of the image she wanted to salvage and which became her in her later twenties and thirties. She married, and later separated from, a young German millionaire, Gunther Sachs. She made the films she wanted to make with little concern for their mediocrity or distinction. Among the more interesting have been two for Godard, *Le*

Mépris (1963), about the break-up of a marriage – Bardot leaves her husband, a writer, and goes off with the American producer (Jack Palance) who employs him. Godard and Bardot concede some nude shots. She also made a brief entry in his *Masculin-Féminin*. She has appeared in Malle's film, *Viva Maria!* (1965, shot in Mexico, with Jeanne Moreau), in which she plays the daughter of an Irish anarchist: the two women form a travelling entertainment, doing striptease and finally leading a revolution. She returned to Malle to play in his episode for the composite film, *Histoires Extraordinaires* (1968), *William Watson*, adapted from Edgar Allen Poe. In 1968 she went to Spain to star in a British-sponsored period 'Western', *Shalako*, directed by Edward Dmytryk, with Sean Connery. She has also appeared on television, playing her guitar, and made disc recordings. On television she wore blue jeans and a sweater, her hair tousled.

The phenomenal success of the Bardot myth, like that of James Dean which just preceded it, was very much the immediate response of the youth public to a need they felt in themselves and which Bardot was the first young girl to realize on the screen. It is François Truffaut – who has, however, not yet directed her – who has said, 'BB is magnificent. More than an actress, she is a person. She symbolizes the period in which we live, identifying herself with a rare realism with all the people with whom we come in contact, and for these reasons I consider her to be unique.'

In 1960 Simone de Beauvoir published her essay, 'Brigitte Bardot and the Lolita Syndrome'; in it she complains that with the social

Right With Jean Gabin in *En cas de Malheur* (1958). He soon gave in to this sort of invitation.

Below Bardot in *La Vérité* (1960), a court-room drama directed by Henri-Georges Clouzot.

Above The love scenes with Jean-Louis Trintignant in *Et Dieu Créa la Femme* (1956) were passionate — and it was suggested that they continued in real life.

Left Bardot in *La Femme et le Pantin* (1959), directed by Julien Duvivier.

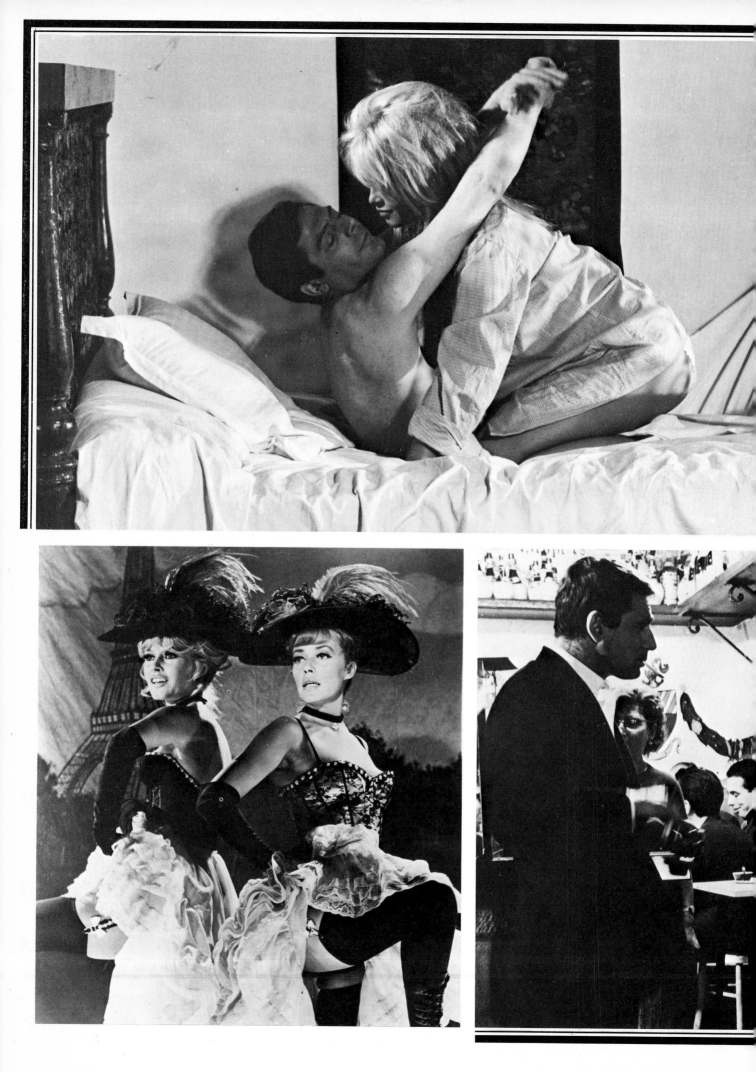

equalizing of men and women in the 1940s and the consequent passing of the old-fashioned vamp, film-makers were forced to seek other provocations for the male and found them in the nymphet, the erotic girls of 12, 13 and 14, the age of female puberty. Girls as young as this were still forbidden to men. 'Bardot is the most perfect specimen of these ambiguous nymphs,' she wrote. 'Seen from behind, her slender, muscular, dancer's body is almost androgynous. Femininity triumphs in her delightful bosom... her hair-do is that of a negligent waif.' Turning her back on the bourgeois equipment of women, the jewellery and accessories, she goes barefoot, indifferent to appearance, her careless but lascivious walk her only conscious gesture towards men. Yet her bodily exposure seems without calculation. She is not a 'bad' woman, like the vamp, and therein lies her danger. 'When I'm in front of the camera, I'm simply myself,' she said of *Et Dieu créa la Femme*.

'A free woman,' says Simone de Beauvoir, 'is the very contrary of a light woman.' Men are alarmed by this directness, this 'haughty shamelessness', because it forces them to face their own sexuality without the mask of romance or the hypocrisies of male superiority and conquest of the female. It is the men now who are reduced to sexual objects; the girl becomes the aggressor, taking and giving sex without love. From the point of view of the audience, there is nothing left with which to identify, no humanity, only voyeurism. What Simone de Beauvoir, writing in 1960, wants to see is the maturing and humanizing of the Bardot image.

Opposite page, above With Marcello Mastroianni in *Vie Privée* (1962) based on Noël Coward's 'Private Lives'.

Left Bardot in *La Bride sur le Cou* (1961), a comedy for which Vadim took over the direction.

Opposite page, below Brigitte Bardot and Jeanne Moreau played two song-and-dance girls who get involved in a revolution in *Viva Maria!* (1965).

Centre Bardot with Robert Hossein in *Le Repos du Guerrier* (1962), a colour CinemaScope spectacular directed by Rogen Vadim.

Below Bardot and Jane Birkin in *Don Juan . . . Or If Don Juan Were A Woman* (1973).

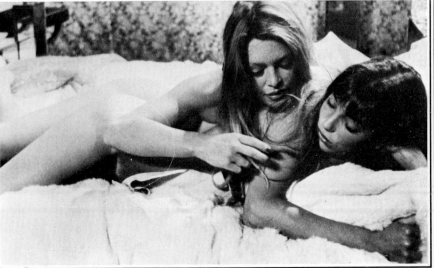

THE NINETEEN SIXTIES AND AFTER

This was a period of fundamental change; faced by the devastating inroads made by television, the cinema responded to the rapidly changing social climate at headlong speed, most notably perhaps in Britain, which achieved a brief reputation in the later 1960s for being 'swinging' and 'permissive'. For a short period America as well as the rest of western Europe seemed to regard London as the principal, even as the notorious, centre for social change. In fact, it was Sweden which had for long been in the van with the easing of censorship, whereas Denmark abandoned it altogether during 1967–69 as far as adults were concerned. Indeed, during the later 1960s the British censors seemed to be leading the general climate of opinion that there was little genuinely adult audiences need be prevented from seeing except the worst excesses of violence, which were present, unhappily, in some American and continental European films, more than in the British. Meanwhile in America the producers'

controlling body, the MPAA, came under a new administration in 1966 with the appointment of Jack Valenti as director, and the inhibiting censorship Code was replaced by an easier system of controls not unlike those in Britain.

It is difficult to say what was most influential in bringing about these radical changes in British-American taste. It was most likely a combination of influences, including pressure by the younger writers and film-makers, a new generation of producers, a more vocal public opposition to the pressure groups which sought to maintain the older restraints in the entertainment media, and the hard commercial need to outflank television, the cinema's keenest competitor. In Britain, both public service and commercial television (which exercise self censorship) led the cinema during the 1960s in abandoning many inhibitions in relation to the handling of sex and in frankness of dialogue. The effective pressure groups in this case were the younger executives, directors and writers

Opposite page Julie Christie, one of the stars of 'permissive' British cinema.

Below Remarkable for her characterization of women in frustrated erotic situations, Glenda Jackson gave one of her most moving performances in *Sunday Bloody Sunday* (1971).

who had general charge of the medium.

This coincided with what came to be termed by the film journalists the 'new wave' movements, primarily in France (where an almost entirely new generation of film-makers dominated the industry briefly about 1960) and to a far less extent in Britain. In America there was not so much a new wave as a new climate favourable to the work of young independent producers and directors who had little time for the inhibitions in subject, treatment and dialogue-writing accepted by their predecessors. In France, the moral as well as the artistic pace was set by influential younger directors such as Vadim, Godard, Resnais, Truffaut, Chabrol and Malle; in Britain it was Anderson, Richardson, Reisz, Schlesinger, Russell, Loach, Boorman, Roeg and the American, Joseph Losey, while in America, the directors of the 1950s already in the forefront in establishing the newer American cinema were supplemented by others, such as Francis Ford Coppola, Peter Bogdanovich, Arthur Hiller, Robert Altman and Mike Nicols. Among the women stars, girls who were setting the pace included Jeanne Moreau and Anna Karina in France, Catherine Deneuve internationally, Sophia Loren, Monica Vitti, and Claudia Cardinale in Italy, Vanessa Redgrave, Sarah Miles, Julie Christie, Maggie Smith, Carol White, and Glenda Jackson in Britain, Ingrid Thulin, Liv Ullman and Harriet and Bibi Andersson in Sweden, and in America, Kim Novak, Jane Fonda, Sue Lyon, Jean Seberg, Natalie Wood, Shirley Knight, Faye Dunaway, Mia Farrow, Raquel Welch, Candice Bergen, Lisa Minelli, Barbra Streisand, Gayle Hunnicutt, Lee Remick and others of the younger generation.

Above Catherine Deneuve with Francis Blanche in *Belle de Jour* (1967) as the frustrated wife who projects her erotic daydreams born of frustration into a situation which represents her as adopting the life of a prostitute.

Right Monica Vitti who starred in a series of films by Antonioni, portrayed women in complex relationships with men. She is seen here in *L'Eclisse* (1962).

Opposite page Gina Lollobrigida was the first of the European sex symbols to become world famous after the Second World War.

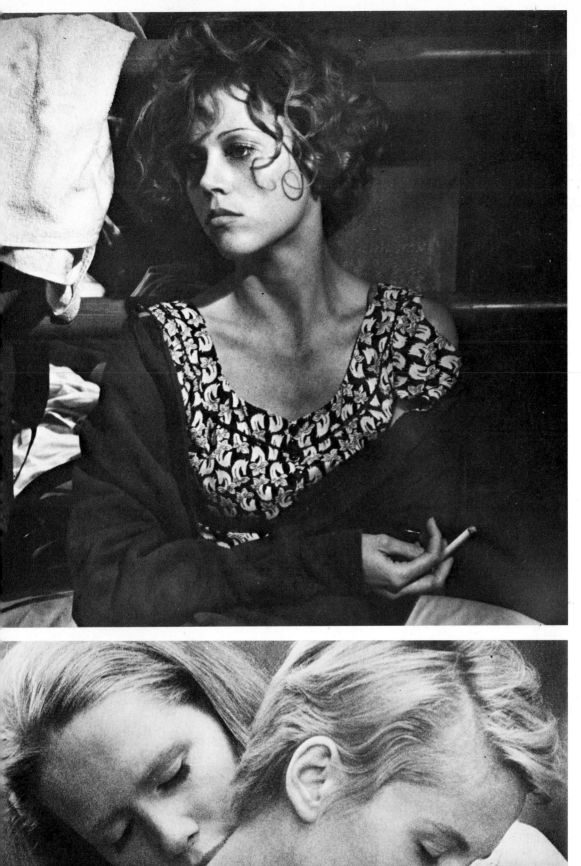

Opposite page Sophia Loren in *Lady L* (1965), a film her husband, Carlo Ponti, made for MGM.

Above Jane Fonda seen here in *They Shoot Horses Don't They?* (1969) represents the emancipated young American actress.

Left Liv Ullman and Bibi Andersson in *Persona* (1967), a psychological film by Bergmann in which the two aspects of a single woman's nature are portrayed by two actresses.

Gina Lollobrigida and Sophia Loren

Gina Lollobrigida was born on 4 July 1927 in a small shop in Subiaco, a mountain town some 50 miles from Rome. She was one of four daughters of a carpenter. During the difficult years of war the family moved to Rome, where Gina eventually won a scholarship to study commercial art. She also posed for the *fumetti* (the Italian picture-story magazines) using the pseudonym Diana Loris, and she won a beauty contest in 1947. Her entry into films resulted from a chance encounter on the street in 1946 with the director, Mario Costa, who offered her a screen test. This led to her initial appearance in the film opera, *Elisir d'Amore* (1946) with Tito Gobbi.

Sophia Loren (Sofia Villani Scicolone) was born on 20 September 1934 in the charity wing of the Santa Margherita Hospital in Rome, but brought up in Pozzuoli, a suburb of Naples. She was the illegitimate daughter of Romilda Villani,* a beautiful woman and a gifted pianist who had always aspired to be an actress. As a child Sophia was used to going barefoot; the family of eight (including her grandparents) had only four rooms, and there were no bathing facilities or hot water in the tenement house they shared with others. Though all the adults in the family worked they became near destitute when Naples was heavily bombed in 1943. After the war, Sophia at the age of only 14 won a beauty contest, and her mother in high hopes took her back to Rome, where they both worked as extras in films from 1950. Sophia also became a model.

Gina Lollobrigida

* Sophia's mother had a potential career in films through her marked resemblance to Garbo, which led to her winning an MGM contest as a double for Garbo in *As You Desire Me* (1932). MGM offered her a contract, but she refused because this meant going to Hollywood. Sophia's father, a travelling salesman called Riccardo Scicolone, was legally recognized as Sophia's father, but though he kept casual contact with Romilda, he never married her or gave much thought to his daughter. Later, Romilda had Sophia's sister Maria by him; she was also to desire to get into films, but she failed.

and she caught the eye of Carlo Ponti, the film producer. He changed her name to Loren, and his special interest in her was to forward her career in films, though at no great speed. She was to play small parts in a number of undistinguished films.

Both Gina Lollobrigida and Sophia Loren appeared in films initially solely on account of their physical beauty. No one thought of them as actresses, a distinction which only came with maturity. To list the films in which they climbed by degrees to stardom would be to list films largely known only in Italy. But gradually they began to attract international attention. The first was Gina Lollobrigida through *Fanfan la Tulipe* (1951, director Christian-Jaque), *Les Belles de Nuit* (1952, director René Clair) – both with Gérard Philipe – and above all through *La Provinciale* (1953, director, Mario Soldati) and the comedy, *Bread, Love and Dreams* (1953, director Luigi Comencini), in which she played a spirited peasant girl opposite Vittorio De

Sica's charming small-town Chief of Police; a sequel, *Bread, Love and Jealousy* was made in 1955 after she had won the Italian Oscar (the Silver Ribbon) for her performance in the first film. In *La Provinciale* she had been able to dub the sound-track with her own voice, which up to this time had been considered too uncultured to use. She had considerable problems over the proper development of her career, since she was rightly ambitious to be considered more than a 'sex goddess'; however, her serious attempts to interpret Moravia's women in this film and later in *La Romana* (1954; director Luigi Zampa) did not really meet with success. In 1949 she married a refugee Yugoslav doctor, Milko Skofic, whom she turned into her manager, but she was hamstrung by an exclusive seven-year Hollywood contract with Howard Hughes (RKO) of which he made little use, but which prevented her from working in America over a period of years. But, with her growing importance to Italian films, and the

Sophia Loren

Right In *La Romana* (1954), based on Alberto Moravia's novel, Lollobrigida plays a prostitute.

Below Lollobrigida in Luigi Comencini's *Bread, Love and Jealousy* (1954), one of a series of successful films entitled *Bread, Love and . . .*

adulation she excited in the Italian public as their outstanding Cinderella, she took great pains to educate herself, acquiring foreign languages so that her renowned beauty could help in the promotion of Italian films by visits abroad as one of the industry's ambassadors.

Her ambition by now was to launch herself as an international star, making films only in English, though her greatest success in Italy was the highly commercial *La Donna più Bella del Mondo*, with Vittorio Gassmann. Held back by the restricting contract with Hughes (which prevented her working in Hollywood for anyone else) she started on her various attempts to become international with such very indifferent films, made in Europe, as *Beat the Devil* (1954; director John Huston, with Humphrey Bogart), *Trapeze* (1956; director Carol Reed, with Burt Lancaster and Tony Curtis), the French version

Above Gina Lollobrigida played a dual role in *Le Grand Jeu* (1953), directed by Robert Siodmak.

Left Gina Lollobrigida as the beautiful gipsy dancer Esmeralda in *The Hunchback of Notre Dame* (1956).

Above Eleanora Brown played Loren's daughter in *Two Women* (*La Ciociara*) (1960), based on Moravia's story in which they were both raped.

Above right With Harry Andrews in *Solomon and Sheba* (1959), a King Vidor film made in Spain.

of *The Hunchback of Notre Dame* (1957: director Jean Delannoy, with Anthony Quinn), and *Solomon and Sheba* (1959; director King Vidor, with Yul Brynner).

She lost the opportunity to appear in Hollywood in *Lady L* with George Cukor, and Sophia Loren eventually won this part, working with Peter Ustinov. But she appeared with Rock Hudson in *Come September* (1961) and *Strange Bedfellows* (1965), with Sean Connery in *Woman of Straw* (1964), with Alec Guinness in *Hotel Paradiso* (1966), and with James Mason in *Bad Man's River* (1972). She has had no shortage of work, and no shortage of talented co-stars or of skilled directors in both wholly Italian and international productions. But the fact remains, she has never achieved the reputation of being a great actress, though as an off-screen personality, and as one of Italy's cultural ambassadors abroad, she has had distinct success, while in Italy itself her Cinderella-like career matches that of Sophia Loren. She was divorced in 1966, and the men with whom her name has from time to time been linked have included Dr Christiaan Barnard.

The pattern of Sophia Loren's career is not at all dissimilar, though her recognition as an actress has risen somewhat higher largely because of the Oscar she won (along with other notable awards) in 1962 for *Two Women*, produced by Carlo Ponti and directed by De Sica. She has a warmer, more sympathetic personality than Gina Lollobrigida; she smiles

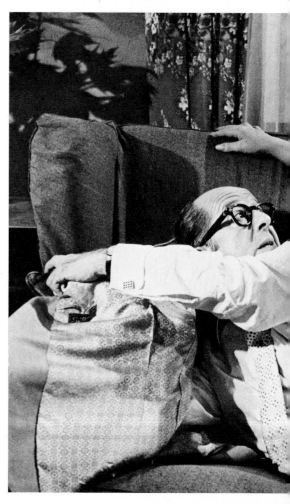

when Gina tends to scowl or pout. But after appearing in many small parts, and working as a model for the *fumetti*, she was noticed internationally for her appearance as a warm-hearted Neapolitan girl in De Sica's episodic *L'Oro di Napoli* (1954). Like Gina Lollobrigida she set about learning languages seriously, notably French and English, and (after she had appeared in Gina's place in the third of the *Bread and Love* films) she was pressed by Ponti to follow the older star into American films. For Hollywood she worked with Cary Grant and Frank Sinatra in *The Pride and the Passion* (1957) – made in Europe – with John Wayne in *Legend of the Lost* (1957), with Clark Gable in *It Started in Naples* (1960), and much more ambitiously with Burl Ives and Anthony Perkins in *Desire under the Elms* (1958), for which her talents unfortunately proved to be scarcely adequate.

It was in 1957 that her controversial Mexican marriage with Carlo Ponti took place, formalized by proxy while she was in America. The Vatican subsequently denounced the marriage as bigamous, refusing to recognize Ponti's divorce. The Mexican marriage had to be accepted as invalid in Italy, and Ponti was driven to take French nationality (as other Italians in similar difficulty have done). The couple were formally remarried in 1966, and after many miscarriages, Sophia gave birth to her child in 1969 and event given much publicity in the world's newspapers.

Like Gina, Sophia was forced in the end to

Below left Vamping Phil Silvers in *Buona Sera Mrs Campbell* (1968), a comedy Lollobrigida made in Hollywood.

Below Sophia Loren and Marcello Mastroianni in *Too Bad She's Bad* (1954).

Above Loren plays a prostitute who ultimately marries Marcello Mastroianni in *Marriage Italian Style* (1964).

Above right Sophia Loren as Lucilla with Stephen Boyd in Samuel Bronston's *The Fall of the Roman Empire* (1964).

Right Loren and Gregory Peck take cover in Stanley Donen's *Arabesque* (1966), an intrigue between rival Arab groups set in London.

orego any aspirations she might have had of becoming a great Hollywood star. But her compensations were many. Her beauty placed her in a class of her own, while her marriage to Carlo Ponti became one of the outstanding romances of film history. He gave her a wonderful mansion to live in, crowning her career as Italy's most enviable Cinderella. Her palace is an historic villa of 50 rooms near Rome which has cost Ponti approaching a million pounds to reconstruct and furnish with the choicest antiques. It has 20 acres of grounds, and a fine swimming-pool. 'Neither before nor since I met Carlo Ponti have I belonged to any other man,' Sophia has said. 'With him I am at peace, a complete woman.' In addition she won her Oscar for *Two Women* (*La Ciociara*, 1961, directed by De Sica, with Jean-Paul Belmondo). Her subsequent films have added little but popular success to this happy climax to her career – putting her for a while into the $1 million a picture class of star – among the better being, perhaps, the De Sica episode in *Boccaccio 70* (1962) and the French film, *Madame Sans-Gêne* (1962), and she lent charm to Chaplin's disastrous *A Countess from Hong Kong* (1967). In 1969 she was awarded the Golden Globe by the US Press Association Foreign Corps, given for the world's most popular woman star.

Above Loren as a peasant girl in Francesco Rosi's *Cinderella, Italian Style* (1967), entitled *More Than A Miracle* in the USA.

Elizabeth Taylor

Elizabeth Taylor was born on 27 February 1932 in London. She and her brother Howard lived until the age of seven in England; her father, the art dealer Francis Taylor, and her mother, the former actress, Sara Sothern, were American. With the onset of the war in Europe they moved to Pasadena, California, where Elizabeth appeared as a child actress in such films as *Lassie Come Home*, *Jane Eyre*, and *The White Cliffs of Dover*. Her English accent and exceptional horsemanship won her the lead in *National Velvet* (1944). As a result, she was put under contract to MGM, and remained so until she appeared in *Cleopatra* (1963).

So she came under the control of Louis B. Mayer, whom she describes eloquently: 'You felt his vitality, but you also felt his enormous arrogance, his ego, his overbearing, driving personality. To know him was to be terrified of him.' She was also much in awe of the great actors and actresses she met around the studio, Katharine Hepburn, Clark Gable, Spencer Tracy, and Judy Garland. She was, she has said, 'constricted by shyness.' Educated from the age of ten in the special MGM classroom, she became a nervous, rather isolated child, unable (because of her unique value) to make the slightest decision without seeking advice or permission.

By the age of 16 she claims she was paid about $2,000 a week, and she looked old enough to play Robert Taylor's wife in *Conspirator* (1949). A child-woman, she played love scenes and studied arithmetic at the same time – she was (as she put it) an emotional child inside a woman's body. To escape into a more normal life, she married in 1950, at the age of 18, Conrad Nicholas Hilton Junior (of the Hilton hotels family), entering the Catholic Church in the process. It was, according to her own account, a marriage doomed from the start; she separated almost at once, but lived apart from her parents, developed ulcers and nervous prostration, and was soon divorced. She describes the experience of this immature marriage as 'horrendous'. She appeared in other films – *Father of the Bride* (1950), *A Place in the Sun* (1951), *Ivanhoe* (1952) – and then in 1952 at the age of 20 sought refuge in a second marriage, this time to Michael Wilding, 20 years older than herself, who represented 'tranquillity, security, maturity'. There were two sons born of this very happy marriage, Michael and Christopher, both Caesarean births. But Elizabeth is accident prone – indeed, this has become part of her myth – and while filming *Elephant Walk* (1954) she suffered an accident which nearly resulted in the loss of an eye.

By now, in 1954, she had appeared in over 20 films; none so far had been demanding in acting, except (when she was 19) *A Place in the Sun* (1951), with Montgomery Clift, a 'Method'

actor. Based on Theodore Dreiser's novel, 'An American Tragedy', it was produced and directed by George Stevens. Elizabeth played the rich girl with whom the poor boy, George Eastman, falls in love. Faced with the concentrated intensity of Clift's acting, Elizabeth, who had never been formally trained, succeeded in giving a sincerely felt, *ingénue* performance. It was the first time she had worked with a highly emotional actor, an experience she was later to repeat with Richard Burton.

George Stevens managed to prise her out of MGM for his Warners production, *Giant* (1956) in this at the age of 23, she had to portray a woman with an age range of 18 to 50. She stood up admirably to this demand, playing a full scale character role in a cast which also starred Rock Hudson and James Dean. During the course of filming she developed trouble with her back, due to sciatica.

After five years of marriage, she had an amicable divorce from Michael Wilding in 1957, and in the same year married 50-year-old Mike Todd. Born in Minneapolis, he was the millionaire son of an impoverished Polish rabbi and he had made a fortune by the age of 19. Unlike others, she found him not loud and vulgar, but tender, sensitive, and in his own way cultivated, though entirely self-educated. She was married after starring in Edward Dmytryk's *Raintree Country* (1957), a film of the Civil War period shot in Kentucky. The part was one of the first in which she had to play a distraught girl. Immediately before her marriage Elizabeth sustained a second severe accident which necessitated removing three discs from her spine, involving great pain. She married Mike Todd after leaving hospital.*

Her own account of her 13-month relationship with this unique man is significant. One side of him was utterly ruthless, the young, dominating tycoon, whose energy never relaxed, and whose sheer love of life never diminished. Like her, he had a swift, devastating temper. In business, she compared him to an octopus, handling telephones, dictaphones, several lines of business all at once. He loaded her with presents, including her first, really outsized diamond ring. But in him her own difficult temperament met its match; she challenged him, she says, because she wanted him to dominate her. When he put her down, she would 'start to purr'. She says he rid her of her inferiority complex, gave her confidence, made her feel 'interesting', overcame her 'constipated' shyness. Elizabeth's public-private life had begun, initially as part of Mike Todd's instinct for showmanship and love of priming the press with stories as they toured the world together promoting his new film, *Around the World in Eighty Days*. They put on acts of violent quarrel, fun rows, because rumours of imminent divorce excited the pressmen.

It was only illness that prevented Elizabeth from flying with her husband on 21 March 1958 to New York to attend his 'Showman of the Year' celebrations. The weather was foul, and his executive plane crashed. Mike Todd's

With James Dean in George Stevens's *Giant* (1956), from Edna Ferber's novel.

She is one of the most amazing women of our time – really a modern Cleopatra.'

Cleopatra (1963; final director, Joseph L Mankiewicz), although dogged with misfortune, was to be a turning-point in her career as an actress, as a woman, and as a legend.* The film was planned to be made largely in England, where Elizabeth and Eddie arrived at the end of August 1960, after endless delays owing to production difficulties. By October she was ill with a virus infection and off work until the following January, when the first director, Rouben Mamoulian resigned. The new director, Mankiewicz, felt it necessary to rescript the film, and set about doing this himself.

Elizabeth, meanwhile, had been staying in a double suite at the Dorchester with husband, children, servants, dogs, and cats ('living like royalty', says Wanger). She had trouble with the press, who antagonized her because of their constant criticism of her. Then in March she fell gravely ill with staphylococcus pneumonia and nearly died. Her life was saved only by tracheotomy and automatic respiration. World reaction, according to Wanger, was unbeliev-

funeral in Chicago was turned into a raree show by certain of Elizabeth's fans – 'Liz, Liz. Come out Liz. Let's have a look,' they screamed. She was under sedation, and she barely got away without her car being overturned.

Still only 26, Elizabeth was a widow. Her third marriage had ended in tragedy. Her only relief was work, the film she had already begun before her illness – Tennessee Williams's *Cat on a Hot Tin Roof* (1958; director Richard Brookes), in which she played Maggie opposite Paul Newman. Elizabeth, obsessed by grief, studied Judaism, and was received into the faith. She became a Jewess, Elisheba Rachel. She also turned to close friendship with the singer, Eddie Fisher, one of Mike Todd's intimates, whose marriage was under strain. He was four years older, and this association added another facet to the mythology of the public-private life of Elizabeth Taylor, namely that she broke up marriages. In May 1959 she married Fisher in Las Vegas, but she admits this marriage, too, was untenable.

At the time of the marriage she was having trouble freeing herself from MGM; she had one more film to make for them, *Butterfield 8*, for which she received about $125,000. She hated the film, regarding the girl as a 'sick nymphomaniac', but perversely she received an Academy Award in 1961 for her termagant performance. Meanwhile she had made, independently, *Suddenly Last Summer* (director Joseph L. Mankiewicz, with Katharine Hepburn and Montgomery Clift), a Tennessee Williams subject in which she played another demented woman with a hard, controlled intensity. Then Walter Wanger offered her the title-role in *Cleopatra*. She asked $1 million; in the end she was to receive over $2 million. 'She is worth every penny of it,' said Wanger. He was convinced she was the only star with 'the necessary youth, power and emotion. . . .

* The extraordinary story of the making of this film is told by Walter Wanger in 'My Life with Cleopatra' (1963). He claims 'there was more world interest in *Cleopatra* . . . and its stars – Elizabeth Taylor, Richard Burton, and Rex Harrison – than in any other news event of 1962.' The year 1962 saw the missile crisis in Cuba! The film, budgeted about $6 million in June 1960, became $37 million by March 1963. Production began in Britain in September 1960 under Mamoulian (who quit in January 1961), resumed under Mankiewicz in February, re-resumed in Rome in September 1961, and finished as far as Elizabeth was concerned in July 1962. In spite of its phenomenal costs, in the end it made money.

Left Elizabeth Taylor played her first romantic lead opposite Robert Taylor in *Conspirator* (1950).

Below Taylor played a rich girl in love with the less-well-off Montgomery Clift in *A Place In the Sun* (1951), a tragedy which received critical acclaim.

Above Suddenly Last Summer (1959) was a successful Tennessee Williams vehicle for Elizabeth Taylor.

Above right Elizabeth Taylor in *Butterfield 8* (1960), from John O'Hara's novel, in which she plays a prostitute.

able; letters and cables poured in, but the film had to be postponed for later resumption in Italy. Once recovered, Elizabeth left for Hollywood, returning to Europe in state with her entourage during the summer to occupy a magnificent villa near Rome with seven bedrooms and six bathrooms. Richard Burton now replaced Stephen Boyd as Antony, and arrived in Italy with his wife, Sybil.

Once they began working together, Elizabeth and Burton fell in love. On the set, according to Wanger, you could 'feel the electricity' between them; he feared another emotional and health crisis affecting the production. By February rumours were rife. Burton was 36, highly cultured, a lover of poetry; he was rugged and strong, the son of a Welsh miner. He had a direct approach to women, at once romantic and candid, charming but well capable of putting a woman 'in her place'. 'His strength, experience, and the dreams he opened up' completely fulfilled what Elizabeth felt she needed. The interim marriage with Eddie Fisher (she wore only Mike's wedding-ring) was fading. In February she admitted her feelings to Wanger, and the most tempestuous relationship in the history of film began. The Italian press, among the yellowest in the world, was upon them.

The romance set up repercussions on an international scale; the American press, according to Wanger, referred to it as a 'cancer' which 'will destroy us all'. A Congressman proposed barring the couple from re-entering the United States on moral grounds. But, as the sociologist Hortense Powdermaker has pointed out, a star's moral reputation is closely bound to the nature of her public image. Elizabeth's fabulous romance with Burton only served to enhance her already romantic, rebellious, free-spoken image. The contrast with the fate of Ingrid Bergman little more than ten years before, is obvious. Both Elizabeth and Burton found their value enhanced; Burton rose to some $500,000 a film, and Elizabeth was worth a million. Nevertheless, she was subject to violent attack in, for example, 'Paris Match', 'France Soir' and the Vatican's 'Osservatore della Domenica' which demanded her children be protected from her).* Wanger remained staunch in her defence: 'I have known many women considered to be paragons of virtue. I doubt, however, that many of these women have as strong a code of personal ethics as Elizabeth. . . I believe that Elizabeth is envied by most of the women in the world because she follows woman's true nature – she goes where her heart leads her. Most people don't dare to follow their heart and, in envy, attack those who do.' There were even bomb threats in the studio. Press photographers got into Elizabeth's house disguised as anything from plumbers to priests, and her servants sold scandalous stories about her to the press.

The film over, Elizabeth separated from Eddie Fisher, and went to live in a new house in Gstaad in Switzerland, existing in near

Above With Montgomery Clift again in *Raintree Country* (1957), for which she received an Oscar nomination.

Left Cat on a Hot Tin Roof (1958), another successful adaptation of a Tennessee Williams's play, in which Taylor has an unsatisfactory marriage with Paul Newman.

* During this period she initiated adoption of a nine-month-old girl from Germany (who became Maria Burton) – a cripple found suffering from malnutrition and covered with abscesses. Elizabeth herself was forbidden to have further children after the birth of Lisa.

As *Cleopatra* (1963) in the spectacular production which cost $37 million, the most expensive film ever.

18-carat gold beads and gave her an impressive statuesque appearance.

In her autobiography published in 1965, she says she and Burton loved to ham up quarrels as a sheer exercise for their lungs. Four-letter words flew, and the fights could turn hot; it was all part of love-vitality. They vied equally to please each other. 'My little shrew is inevitably tamed after a bit of talking,' said Burton. 'The most important thing of our marriage is the continual excitement.' She is 'blazingly honest', he has said, and has 'a roaring sense of humour'. He has given her a genuine love for poetry, and they have undertaken occasional public recitals together in recent years.

Owing to the difficulty in insuring Elizabeth's health, she got no further film until *The Sandpiper* (1965; director Vincente Minnelli) for which she was paid her million dollars. The story concerned a love-affair between an Episcopalian minister and a woman painter living a free, unconventional life. The next film represented an advance, *Who's Afraid of Virginia Woolf?* (1966; director Mike Nichols, his first film) in which she and Burton could turn their half-horsing, half-real rows to account in the destructive passion of the quarrelling couple in Albee's play. She played Martha, frustrated wife of a New England professor, as a desperate woman covering her vulnerability by being 'bawdy, sloppy, snarly'. For this performance she won her second Academy Award.

'The Elizabeth Taylor who's famous, the one on celluloid, really has no depth or meaning to me,' she wrote in her memoirs, which are frank, revealing, honest, and touching. She insists she is not a 'sex goddess' or a 'sex symbol'. She admits she and Burton together may well be 'sex symbols . . . because we suggest love'. He has what she calls 'jungle essence'. Beauty in women, she thinks, should have character, have flaws, not look over cared for; and women should not be afraid of age, which can add its own beauty. Her flaws, she says, are that her legs are too short, her arms too long, her hands too big, her body too fat. She and Burton created a marriage which kept them in the public eye for ten years; they separated, reunited, and finally divorced in 1973. Their wealth became fabulous; they could earn between them some $3 million a picture. Their gifts to each other assumed an Arabian Nights lavishness. But, as he has put it, 'we both have feelings of insecurity', though as late as August 1974, in a London 'Times' interview, Burton anticipated they might one day reunite. 'We are flesh of one flesh, bone of one bone,' he said.

Together they had made a lively version of *The Taming of the Shrew* (1967, director Franco Zeffirelli) and the Graham Greene story, *The Comedians* (1967), an indifferent piece. She also appeared (mute) as a Baroque vision of female allure in Burton's own production of Marlowe's *Dr Faustus*. After this, since she was now indulging her independent taste, she appeared

isolation. She was divorced in 1964, and after a period apart began to meet Burton again. His divorce was now inevitable, and they finally married in Montreal in 1964, while Burton was rehearsing 'Hamlet' under John Gielgud's direction. After the marriage they were mobbed by press and public wherever they went in North America, often with insulting questions pressed on them. They had found before their marriage a friendlier reaction in Britain, where they had made the Rattigan-Asquith film, *The VIPS* (1964).

When *Cleopatra* was eventually released and it was found that Rex Harrison's urbane and witty Caesar had virtually stolen the picture, Elizabeth was not slow to express criticism of her performance, though she claimed much of the best of her and Burton's acting had been cut. Her petulance as Cleopatra and Burton's vituperation as Antony did not amount to great acting, but the script, bearing the marks of strain in Mankiewicz's hasty writing, did not offer chances for distinction. The film depended on her physical beauty and on spectacle. Her 60 costumes are said to have cost some $250,000, and the dress she wore for the entry into Rome on a black glass-fibre sphinx was made of

Taylor and Burton in *Who's Afraid of Virginia Woolf?* (1966) as husband and wife who quarrel viciously. She won a second Oscar for her performance.

t intervals in relatively esoteric films – John Huston's *Reflections in a Golden Eye* (1967), based on a story by Carson McCullers, in which she is an errant wife in a claustrophobic army community, and Joseph Losey's two remarkable films, *Boom!* (another Tennessee Williams theme) and *Secret Ceremony* (1968). In the allegorical *Boom!* Burton plays a gigolo-poet, symbolic of Death, who visits a wealthy, tyrannical but still beautiful chatelaine (six times widowed), living isolated on her Mediterranean island. He becomes her last lover, administering the kiss of death. In *Secret Ceremony* she is a prostitute who takes a vampire-like possession of a rich orphan-girl, aged 22. In both roles her fuller desire for acting is fulfilled, but neither were successful at the box-office. With George Stevens's *The Only*

There were more quarrels for Taylor and Burton in *The Taming of the Shrew* (1967), but some tender scenes as well.

Elizabeth Taylor played the wife of Richard Burton in *The VIPs* (1964).

161

Above Elizabeth Taylor and
Brian Keith in *Reflections in
a Golden Eye* (1967).

Game in Town (1969), set in Las Vegas but shot in Paris, she returned to a more Hollywood-styled film, playing a chorus-girl living at odds with a young compulsive gambler (Warren Beatty); this was her last million-dollar film. By now her name had dropped out of the top ten box-office stars.

Her later appearances included the film version of Dylan Thomas's play, *Under Milk Wood* (1971) and Peter Ustinov's black Faustian comedy, *Hammersmith is Out* (1972), both with Burton, as well as the sexually extravagant *Zee and Company* (1971, from a story by Edna O'Brien) and a murder mystery, *Night Watch* (1973), both directed by the American, Brian G. Hutton. In virtually every film of the last few years, Elizabeth seems to have been cast (and latterly to have cast herself) in the role of a woman seeking to dominate men, and on occasion other women. As Alexander Walker has surmised, this may be, in part at least, because as an actress she may seek the fulfilment of private fantasy in the parts she selects. Or is it, less subtly, that she instinctively knows her limitations as a player and realizes she is at her most effective as the beautiful termagant inflicting wounds on herself in wounding others.

Above Mia Farrow lives under the spell of the older Taylor in Joseph Losey's *Secret Ceremony* (1969).

Left Elizabeth Taylor and Peter O'Toole in *Under Milk Wood* (1971).

Jeanne Moreau

Jeanne Moreau is both a modern character actress and, in her own individual style, since the 1960s a representative woman of our time. Her range of films include a few of the more significant of the period; she has worked for Vadim, Malle, Godard, Truffaut, Antonioni, and Ophuls as well as Ritt, Brook, Losey, Welles, and Foreman. In the theatre she started at the Comédie-Française. She followed a career in conventional films throughout the 1950s, before her association with the French 'new wave'. She is by far the most versatile star in post-war French cinema, and along with Bardot the best known internationally.

She was born in Paris on 23 January 1928. Her father owned a restaurant in Montmartre; her mother, a former dancer, Kathleen Buckley, was English, coming from Lancashire. She had been a Tiller girl and had married Anatole Moreau when he was a barman. Jeanne spent part of her childhood with her mother in England, and her English grandfather, whom she loved, was a sailor. She was a happy child, with certain gifts – imagination, and an ability to express herself – and she was bilingual in French and English. But she was somewhat strictly brought up by her father, who opposed her desire after the age of 15 to train for the theatre. In 1939 her parents divorced; she stayed with her father in France, though she was to retain warm relations with her mother in England. Moreau finally permitted his daughter to study for the theatre, but she dates her innate desire for independence from this period. While still a student at the Conservatoire, she was chosen in 1947 to appear as Veroutchka in Turgenev's 'A Month in the Country' at the Comédie-Française, and her success resulted in a four-year contract lasting from 1948 to 1952. At the same time she married in September 1949 a young actor, Jean-Louis Richard, her son Jérôme being born the day after the wedding.

She claims she always knew she was going to be a great star. Nevertheless, she suffered on occasion acute stage-fright, 'an animal fear, utterly bestial'. But 'fear is necessary,' she thinks. 'To be a good actress you have to feel in danger all the time – danger of being bad. To be a really *great* actress you can't be quite normal.' Bored by the work at the Comédie-Française, on the expiration of her contract she joined the Théâtre National Populaire, attracted by the 'fringe' theatre; at the same time she began to appear in films, but her particular kind of beauty – her widely spaced eyes, her broad nose, her capacious, expressive mouth with its downward turn could never be made to conform to standardized beauty treatment. She had to be seen as she was, and her early films did her little credit. But on the stage she achieved further success in an adaptation from Charles Morgan, 'L'Heure Eblouissante', as Liza in Shaw's 'Pygmalion', and above all as the unhappy wife in 'Cat on a Hot Tin Roof' (1956).

Her first notable part in films was as a prostitute in Jacques Becker's *Touchez-pas au Grisby* (1954), but her potentialities as a star in erotic subjects began in *La Reine Margot* (1955). Her screen personality emerged for the first time when her face was at last permitted to appear free from artificial beautification in Malle's *Ascenseur pour l'échafaud* (1957). It was her 21st film, and her coming of age as a screen star, though the film was a conventional thriller. She was 29, and her director 25, making his first feature film after working as assistant to Cousteau. But, as Truffaut put it, Malle 'saw her with new eyes', and she appeared in his next film, *Les Amants* (1958) to far greater advantage, playing the bored wife of a rich provincial. She falls in love overnight with a young student and elopes with him at dawn. She was able to act with a new, concentrated sincerity, at once frank and lyrical. At one moment she had to show this woman experiencing orgasm through oral stimulation, a moment requiring great concentration and, she says, 'very, very hard to do'. But the film was not erotic, she thinks – 'more a social film about the way people live'.

Films now followed on quickly, unequal in quality but including several important in establishing the new cinema in France. Others introduced her to international stardom – *La Notte* (1961; Antonioni), *Eva* (1962; Losey), *The Trial* (1962; Welles), *The Victors* (1963; Foreman), *The Yellow Rolls-Royce* (1964; Asquith), *The Train* (1964; Frankenheimer). In France and in French she made *Les Liaisons Dangereuses* (1959; Vadim) and in 1960 *Moderato Cantabile* for Peter Brook, playing another disillusioned wife with such controlled passion that once again she stole the picture. But it was Truffaut's *Jules et Jim* (1961) that gave her a more enigmatic part; a woman who enters the lives of two men closely bound in friendship, taking complete possession of them. She brings delicacy as well as strength and tenacity to the personality of the woman. She not only helped Truffaut finance the film, she cooked for the total unit of 22 while on location in Alsace. 'We shot it all without sound, just made up the words as we went along, and later dubbed it in ten days,' she said later. She has also revealed her unhappiness while working with Antonioni, 'I felt completely lost in *La Notte*: I speak Italian but there was no communication between Antonioni and me. . . . My mood of depression may have shown on the screen and fitted the film.' In *La Notte* she plays the unfulfilled wife of a once successful writer whose creativity is in a state of crisis.

For a woman of such individuality on the screen, Moreau is strangely recessive when it comes to choosing parts to play. She prefers, she says, to have others choose them for her, which may in part account for her appearance (often in cameo parts) in such unlikely films as *The Victors* and *The Yellow Rolls-Royce*. She enjoys playing small parts in the films of

directors she likes, such as Welles (*The Trial* and *Chimes at Midnight*). In *Eva*, Moreau and Stanley Baker present the troubled relations between a Welshman obsessed with love and a Frenchwoman obsessed with money. The woman sets out to tantalize, madden and humiliate him. Losey says the situation was a statement about a sexual relationship, and the film was dogged by production troubles.

Moreau returned to Malle to play the small part of a drug-addicted artist in *Le Feu Follet* (1963) and *Viva Maria!* (1965), which excited curiosity because she was teamed with Bardot.* However, back in Paris she found another highly compatible director in Buñuel (*The Diary of a Chambermaid*, 1964). In Buñuel's corrosive study she plays the sardonic observer, the servant Célestine who sees and comprehends all that goes on in the wholly corrupt family for whom she works. 'Célestine is Buñuel himself,' she has said, 'the way she watches, critical, humorous. Buñuel has a lot of humour, though it is black humour.' She also played to some extent for humour in a film directed by her former husband, Richard, *Mata-Hari, Agent H21* (1964). She endows the character of the spy with a Baroque complexity, at once neurotic and seductive.

Moreau has also appeared in two idiosyncratic films directed by Tony Richardson, *Mademoiselle* (1966), with a script by Genêt, and *The Sailor from Gibraltar* (1967), from a story by Marguerite Duras, in both of which she plays lonely, frustrated and predatory women; in the first she is an elegantly dressed schoolmistress, who brings destruction by fire and flood to the village where she has her school; in the second, a film with an allegorical twist, she finds a new lover while sailing the seas to rediscover an old one. In 1966 she worked again with Welles in one of his best films, *The Immortal Story*, made originally for French television; a girl uses sex to achieve a ritual vengeance against the rich old man who bankrupted her father. She found another extravagant situation in Truffaut's *La Mariée était en noir* (1967), a film modelled on Hitchcock, in which, clad either wholly in white or in black, she takes a remorseless vengeance in turn on the five men who accidentally shot her bridegroom on the steps of the church.

In 1967 she made another strange choice, appearing in England in a spectacular film version of Bernard Shaw's short play *Great Catherine* (director Gordon Flemying), a vastly over-developed burlesque; she also worked in America, principally on *Monte Walsh* (1970, director William A. Fraker), a down-beat, atmospheric Western in which she plays a saloon hostess. More recently she has appeared in France in several films – in Roger Pigaut's thriller, *Comptes à Rebours* (1970), *L'Humeur Vagabonde* (1971, director Edouard Luntz), *Chère Louise* (1972, director Philippe de Broca) and *Nathalie Grainger* (1973, director Marguerite Duras). She sang in *Le Petit Théâtre de Jean Renoir* (1971, and indeed ever since she sang 'Le Tourbillon' in *Jules et Jim*

* She hated this experience, the exhaustion of working in the rarefied atmosphere of Mexico and discovering her incompatibility with Bardot; she found Bardot's spontaneity false.

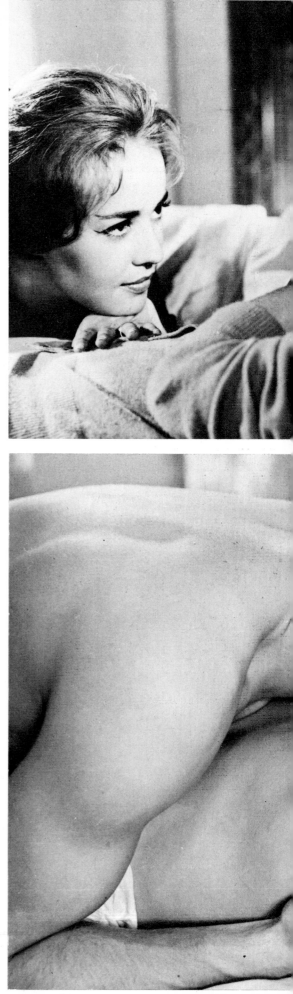

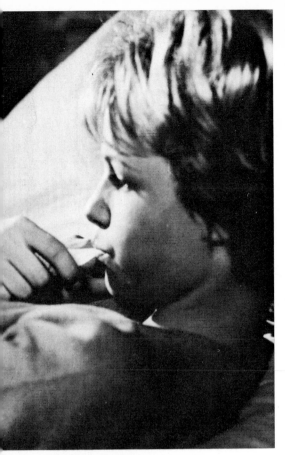

Above Jeanne Moreau providing comfort for Jean Gabin in *Gas-Oil* (1955).

Above left Moreau seduces Annette Stroyberg in *Les Liaisons Dangereuses* (1959) because she suspects Stroyberg of an affair with her husband.

Left In Louis Malle's *Les Amants* (1958), Moreau plays the mistress of Jean-Marc Bory. The film gained her international notice.

Right With Stanley Baker in
Joseph Losey's *Eve* (1962).

Opposite page, above
Moreau and Henri Serre in
Jules and Jim (1961),
Truffant's film of Henri-
Pierre Roche's novel, in
which Moreau dominated the
lives of two men who were
close friends.

she has developed a subsidiary career as a
singer and recording artist.

Jeanne Moreau's stardom has obviously
rested more in her personality than in the
distinction of the films in which she has mostly
appeared. But acting for her is therapeutic: 'I
wanted to act because I wanted to be different.
If I wasn't an actress I might have been an
hysteric. Acting isn't a profession; it's an
extension of oneself. When I work, every part
of me is involved. . . . Playing is an instinctive
need.' Her strange, highly individual mingling
of remoteness with sensuality, her brooding
melancholy, create a powerful image in the
most indifferent films. But, like certain other
stars, she has built an off-screen reputation for
independence. Recently she was among the 342
actresses, writers and other prominent French-
women who signed a statement they had
obtained abortions, which is against a law in
France they were campaigning to have
abolished. 'I am a sensualist who believes that
what makes me feel good cannot possibly be
bad,' she has said.

She has had to put up with public criticism
of her way of life, and although a nervous
woman, especially when facing up to a demanding part, she believes in frankness, acknow-
ledges the identity of lovers, such as Louis
Malle and Pierre Cardin, and believes that
former lovers, like her ex-husband, may remain
as lifelong friends. Her view of women's
emancipation is 'to be balanced in leading our
life – that is the only emancipation'. She claims
to be deeply religious. The great virtue, she

Right Moreau in Antonioni's
La Notte (1961), in which
she played the disorientated
wife of a celebrated novelist.

Opposite page, below
Moreau at the roulette-table
in *La Baie des Anges* (1963).
She played a compulsive
gambler.

Above In Carl Foreman's *The Victors* (1963) with Eli Wallach. She plays a victim of the war.

Right Jeanne Moreau in *Mademoiselle* (1965), directed by Tony Richardson from Jean Genet's story.

maintains, is self-control, to spare oneself and others suffering. In a 'Life' interview, given when she was approaching 40, she is quoted as saying, 'I have such curiosity, such a tender curiosity about the vulnerable mystery a man is,' and spoke of 'that violent combination of passion and tenderness I so much need. . . . Sensuality, for me, is a notion of joy, of happiness, of fulfilment. . . . A man who looks at a woman and finds her sensuous sees in that woman a promise of harmony. A man who looks at a woman and finds her sexy – what a horrible word – changes that woman into an object, a bit of merchandise. Instead of a dialogue, it's an instant-long appetite, a stupidity. . . . I emerge from a successful love affair a larger person. . . . Each woman is granted a certain store of love force. There's only a few she can love deeply.' 'I think,' she has said, 'my life has been radical and honest, compared with the hypocrisy of most women. I've been a nonconformist, my own mistress.'

She claims to have no political opinions, no

ormally held ideas, but she has always been a reat reader since childhood. In the early 1960s he acquired her own villa and estate on the ôte d'Azur, near Saint-Tropez. By 1965 she ould command $120,000 for a French film, plus 5 per cent of the profits.

During the 1960s she conceived the ambition o play Shakespeare's Cleopatra, an idea suggested by Peter Brook. There could be no more deal casting for this small, brilliant, volatile, nd wholly contemporary woman.

Above Jeanne Moreau in Luis Buñuel's remake of *Diary of a Chambermaid* (1964).

Left Moreau in *Viva Maria!* (1965).

Arletty

Les Perles de la Couronne. 1937. Sacha Guitry. With Guitry, Raimu, Marcel Dalio, Jean-Louis Barrault

Hôtel du Nord. 1938. Marcel Carné. With Annabella, Louis Jouvet, Jean-Pierre Aumont

Fric-Frac. 1939. Claude Autant-Lara. With Michel Simon, Fernandel

Le Jour se lève. 1939. Marcel Carné. With Jean Gabin, Jules Berry, Jacqueline Laurent

Les Visiteurs du Soir. 1942. Marcel Carné. With Jules Berry, Marie Déa, Fernand Ledoux, Alain Cuny

Les Enfants du Paradis. 1944. Marcel Carné. With Jean-Louis Barrault, Pierre Brasseur, Maria Casarès, Gaston Modot, Pierre Renoir, Louis Salou, Jane Marken

Huis-Clos. 1954. Jacqueline Audry. With Gaby Sylvia

The Longest Day. 1961. Twentieth Century-Fox. Co-directors Andrew Marton, Ken Annakin, Bernhard Wicki, Gerd Oswald. With Jean-Louis Barrault, André Bourvil

Theda Bara

Unless otherwise stated, the production Company was Fox.

A Fool There Was. 1915. Production, Box Office Attractions. Frank Powell. With Edward Jose, Mabel Frenyer

The Kreutzer Sonata. 1915. Herbert Brennon. With Nance O'Neil, William E. Shay, Henry Bergman

East Lynne. 1916. Bertram

Bracken. With Ben Deely, Stuart Holmes, Claire Whitney

Romeo and Juliet. 1916. J. Gordon Edwards. With Harry Hilliard, Glen White

Camille. 1917. J. Gordon Edwards. With Albert Roscoe

Cleopatra. 1917. J. Gordon Edwards. With Fritz Leiber (Caesar), Thurston Hall (Antony)

Madame Dubarry. 1918. J. Gordon Edwards. With Charles Clary, Fred Church

The Soul of Buddha. 1918. J. Gordon Edwards Scripted by Theda Bara. With Hugh Thompson

Salome. 1918. J. Gordon Edwards. With G. Raymond Nye (Herod), Albert Roscoe (John the Baptist)

Kathleen Mavourneen. 1919. Charles J. Mavourneen. With Edward O'Connor, Jennie Dickenson

Brigitte Bardot

Et Dieu Crèa la Femme. 1956. Roger Vadim. With Curt Jurgens, Jean-Louis Trintignant, Christian Marquand

La Lumière d'en Face. 1955. Georges Lacombe. With Raymond Pellegrin, Roger Pigaut

En cas de Malheur (Love is my Profession). 1958. Claude Autant-Lara. With Jean Gabin, Edwige Feuillère

La Vérité. 1960. Henri-Georges Clouzot. With Sami Frey, Marie-José Nat, Charles Vanel, Paul Meurisse

La Vie Privée. 1961. Louis Malle. With Marcello Mastroianni

Viva Maria! 1965. Louis Malle. With Jeanne Moreau, George Hamilton

Ingrid Bergman

Intermezzo. 1936. Svensk-Filmindustri. Gustav Molander. With Gosta Ekman

Intermezzo. 1939. United Artists. Gregory Ratoff. With Leslie Howard, Edna Best

Dr Jekyll and Mr Hyde. 1941. MGM. Victor Fleming. With Spencer Tracy, Lana Turner, Ian Hunter, Donald Crisp, C. Aubrey Smith, Sara Allgood

Casablanca. 1942. Warner Bros. Michael Curtiz. With Humphrey Bogart, Paul Henreid, Claude Rains, Conrad Veidt, Sydney Greenstreet, Peter Lorre

For Whom The Bell Tolls. 1943. Paramount. Sam Wood. With Gary Cooper, Akim Tamiroff, Katina Paxinou

Gaslight. 1944. MGM. George Cukor. With Joseph Cotton, Charles Boyer, Dame May Whitty, Angela Lansbury

Spellbound. 1945. United Artists. Alfred Hitchcock. With Gregory Peck, Michael Chekhov, Leo G. Carroll

Notorious. 1946. RKO. Alfred Hitchcock. With Cary Grant, Claude Rains, Louis Calhern

Joan of Arc. 1948. RKO. Victor Fleming. With José Ferrer, George Coulouris

Stromboli. 1950. RKO. Roberto Rossellini. With Mario Vitale, Renzo Cesana, Mario Sponza

Europa '51. 1952. Ponti-De Laurentiis. Roberto Rossellini. With Alexander Knox, Giulietta Masina

We the Women (Ingrid Bergman; third episode). 1953. Roberto Rossellini. With Albamarie Setaccioli

Journey to Italy (The Lonely Woman). 1953. Roberto Rossellini. With George Sanders

Joan at the Stake. 1954. Roberto Rossellini. With Tullio Carminati

Anastasia. 1957. Fox. Anatole Litvak. With Yul Brynner, Helen Hayes, Akim Tamiroff, Felix Aylmer, Martita Hunt, Sacha Pitoëff, Ivan Desny

Indiscreet. 1958. Warner Bros. Stanley Donen. With Cary Grant, Cecil Parker, Phyllis Calvert, David Kossoff

Inn of the Sixth Happiness. 1958. Fox. Mark Robson. With Curt Jurgens, Robert Donat

Aimex-vous Brahms? (Goodbye Again). 1961. United Artists. Anatole Litvak. With Yves Montand Anthony Perkins, Jessie Royce Landis

Clara Bow

Unless otherwise stated, the production Company was Paramount.

Black Oxen. 1924. First National. Frank Lloyd. With Corinne Griffith, Conway Tearle

Kiss Me Again. 1925. Warner Bros. Ernst Lubitsch. With Marie Prevost, Monte Blue, John Roche

The Plastic Age. 1925. Preferred. Wesley Ruggles. With Donald Keith, Mary Alden, Henry B. Walthall, Clark Gable (supporting)

My Lady of Whims. 1926. Arrow. Dallas M. Fitzgerald With Donald Keith, Carmelita Geraghty, Lee Moran

Mantrap. 1926. Victor Fleming. With Ernest Torrence, Percy Marmont, Eugene Pallette

Kid Boots. 1926. Frank Tuttle. With Eddie Cantor, Billie Dove

Dancing Mothers. 1926. Herbert Brenon. With Alice Joyce, Conway Tearle, Donald Keith, Dorothy Cumming

It. 1927. Clarence Badger. With Antonio Moreno, William Austin, Elinor Glyn, Gary Cooper (supporting)

Wings. 1927. William A. Wellman. With Charles 'Buddy' Rogers, Richard Arlen, Gary Cooper, Henry B. Walthall, Hedda Hopper

Red Hair. 1928. Clarence Badger. With Lane Chandler, Laurence Grant, William Austin

Dangerous Curves. 1929. Lothar Mendes. With Richard Arlen, Kay Francis

Love among the Millionaires. 1930. Frank Tuttle. With Stanley Smith, Skeets Gallagher

Joan Crawford

Unless otherwise stated, the production Company was MGM.

Sally, Irene and Mary. 1925. Metro-Goldwyn. Edmund Goulding. With Constance Bennett, Sally O'Neil, William Haines

The Unknown. 1927. Tod Browning. With Lon Chaney

Our Dancing Daughters. 1928. Harry Beaumont. With Johnny Mack Brown, Dorothy Sebastian, Anita Page, Nils Asther

Our Modern Maidens. 1929. Jack Conway. With Rod La Rocque, Douglas Fairbanks Junior, Anita Page

Hollywood Revue. 1929. Charles Reisner. With all-star cast

Paid. 1930. Sam Wood. With Robert Armstrong, Marie Prevost

Dance, Fools, Dance. 1931. Harry Beaumont. With William Holden, Clark Gable, Lester Vail

Laughing Sinners. 1931. Harry Beaumont. With Neil Hamilton, Clark Gable

This Modern Age. 1931. Nicholas Grinde. With Pauline Frederick, Neil Hamilton

Grand Hotel. 1932. Edmund Goulding. With Greta Garbo, Wallace Beery, John Barrymore, Lionel Barrymore

Rain. 1932. United Artists. Lewis Milestone. With Walter Huston

Dancing Lady. 1933. Robert Z. Leonard. With Clark Gable, Franchot Tone, Fred Astaire

No More Ladies. 1935. George Cukor; Edward H. Griffith. With Robert Montgomery, Charlie Ruggles, Franchot Tone

The Gorgeous Hussy. 1936. Clarence Brown. With Robert Taylor, Lionel Barrymore, Franchot Tone, Melvyn Douglas, James Stewart

The Women. 1939. George Cukor. With Norma Shearer, Rosalind Russell, Mary Boland, Paulette Goddard, Joan Fontaine

Strange Cargo. 1940. Frank Borzage. With Clark Gable, Ian Hunter, Peter Lorre, Paul Lukas

Susan and God (The Gay Mrs Trexel) 1940. George Cukor. With Fredric March, Rita Hayworth

A Woman's Face. 1941. George Cukor. With Melvyn Douglas, Conrad Veidt

Mildred Pierce. 1945. Warner Bros. Michael Curtiz. With Jack Carson, Zachary Scott, Eve Arden

Humoresque. 1946. Warner Bros. Jean Negulesco. With Joan Garfield

Harriet Craig. 1950. Columbia. Vincent Sherman. With Wendell Corey

Johnny Guitar. 1954. Republic. Nicholas Ray. With Sterling Hayden, Mercedes McCambridge, Scott Brady

The Story of Esther Costello. 1957. Columbia. David Miller. With Rossano Brazzi, Heather Sears

Whatever Happened to Baby Jane? 1962. Warner Bros. Robert Aldrich. With Bette Davis.

Marlene Dietrich

Unless otherwise stated, the production Company was Paramount.

The Blue Angel. 1930. UFA. Josef von Sternberg. With Emil Jannings, Hans Albers

Morocco. 1930. Josef von Sternberg. With Gary Cooper, Adolphe Menjou

Dishonoured. 1931. Josef von Sternberg. With Victor McLaglen, Lew Cody, Warner Oland

Shanghai Express. 1932. Josef von Sternberg. With Clive Brook, Anna May Wong, Warner Oland, Eugene Pallette

Blonde Venus. 1932. Josef von Sternberg. With Herbert Marshall, Cary Grant

Song of Songs. 1933. Rouben Mamoulian. With Brian Aherne, Lionel Atwill, Alison Skipworth

The Scarlet Empress. 1934. Josef von Sternberg. With John Lodge, Sam Jaffe, C. Aubrey Smith

The Devil is a Woman. 1935. Josef von Sternberg. With Lionel Atwill, Cesar Romero. Edward Everett Horton, Alison Skipworth

Desire. 1936. Ernst Lubitsch. With Gary Cooper, John Halliday, Akim Tamiroff, Alan Mobray

Destry Rides Again. 1939. Universal-International. George Marshall. With James Stewart, Charles Winniger, Brian Donlevy, Una Merkel

The Flame of New Orleans. 1941. Universal-International. René Clair. With Roland Young, Bruce Cabot

A Foreign Affair. 1948. Billy Wilder. With Jean Arthur, John Lund, Millard Mitchell

Stage Fright. 1950. Warners. Alfred Hitchcock. With Jane Wyman, Richard Todd, Michael Wilding

Witness for the Prosecution. 1957. United Artists. Billy Wilder. With Tyrone Power, Charles Laughton, Elsa Lanchester

Touch of Evil. 1958. Universal-International. Orson Welles. With Charlton Heston, Janet Leigh, Orson Welles, Joseph Calleia, Akim Tamiroff

Judgment at Nuremberg. 1962. United Artists. Stanley Kramer. With Spencer Tracy, Burt Lancaster, Richard Widmark, Maximilian Schell, Judy Garland, Montgomery Clift

Greta Garbo

Unless otherwise stated, the production Company was MGM.

The Atonement of Gosta Berling. 1924. Svensk Filmindustri. Mauritz Stiller. With Lars Hanson. (Garbo has starring role in this, her first feature film)

The Joyless Street. 1925. Sofar Film. G. W. Pabst. With Werner Krauss, Asta Nielsen, Valeska Gert

Flesh and the Devil. 1927. Clarence Brown. With John Gilbert, Lars Hanson

Love. 1927. Edmund Goulding. With John Gilbert, George Fawcett

The Divine Woman. 1928. Victor Seastrom. With Lars Hanson, Lowell Sherman, Polly Moran

The Kiss. 1929. Jacques Feyder. With Conrad Nagel, Anders Randolf, Lew Ayres

Anna Christie. 1930. Clarence Brown. With Charles Bickford, Marie Dressler

Mata Hari. 1932. George Fitzmaurice. With Ramon Novarro, Lionel Barrymore, Lewis Stone

Grand Hotel. 1932. Edmund Goulding. With John Barrymore, Joan Crawford, Wallace Beery, Lionel Barrymore, Jean Hersholt

Queen Christina. 1933. Rouben Mamoulian. With John Gilbert, Ian Keith, Lewis Stone, C. Aubrey Smith

Anna Karenina. 1935. Clarence Brown. With Fredric March, Freddie Bartholomew, Maureen O'Sullivan, May Robson, Basil Rathbone

Camille. 1936. George Cukor. With Robert Taylor, Lionel Barrymore, Elizabeth Allan

Ninotchka. 1939. Ernst Lubitsch. With Melvyn Douglas, Ina Claire, Sig Rumann, Alexander Granach, Bela Lugosi

Two-Faced Woman. 1941. George Cukor. With Melvyn Douglas, Constance Bennett, Roland Young, Robert Sterling

Betty Grable

Unless otherwise stated, the production company was Twentieth Century-Fox.

Million Dollar Legs. 1939. Paramount. Nick Grinde. With John Hartley, Donald O'Connor, Jackie Coogan

Down Argentine Way. 1940. Irving Cummings. With Don Ameche, Carmen Miranda, Charlotte Greenwood, J. Carroll Naish

Tin Pan Alley. 1940. Walter Lang. With Alice Faye, Jack Oakie, Esther Ralston, John Loder

A Yank in the RAF. 1941. Henry King. With Tyrone Power, John Sutton, Reginald Gardiner, Donald Stuart

Pin-up Girl. 1944. H. Bruce Humberstone. With John Harvey, Martha Raye, Joe E. Brown, Eugene Pallette

The Dolly Sisters. 1945. Irving Cummings. With John Payne, June Haver, Reginald Gardiner

Mother Wore Tights. 1947. Walter Lang. With Dan Dailey, Mona Freeman, Connie Marshall

When My Baby Smiles at Me. 1948. Walter Lang. With Dan Dailey, Jack Oakie, June Havoc, Richard Arlen, James Gleason

The Beautiful Blonde from Bashful Bend. 1949. Preston Sturges. With Cesar Romero, Rudy Vallee

How to Marry a Millionaire. 1953. Jean Negulesco. With Marilyn Monroe, Lauren Bacall, David Wayne, William Powell

Jean Harlow

Double Whoopee. 1929. MGM. Lewis Foster. With Laurel and Hardy

Hell's Angels. 1929. United Artists. Howard Hughes and James Whale. With Ben Lyon and James Hall

The Love Parade. 1930. Paramount. Ernst Lubitsch. With Maurice Chevalier, Jeanette MacDonald, Ben Turpin, Lionel Barrymore

Public Enemy. 1931. Warner Brothers. William Wellman. With James Cagney, Joan Blondell

Platinum Blond (e). 1931. Columbia. Frank Capra. With Robert Williams, Loretta Young

Red Dust. 1932. MGM. Victor Fleming. With Clark Gable, Donald Crisp

Bombshell [Blonde Bombshell]. 1933. MGM. Victor Fleming. With Franchot Tone.

Dinner at Eight. 1933. MGM. George Cukor. With John Barrymore, Marie Dressler, Lionel Barrymore, Wallace Beery, Jean Hersholt

Libelled Lady. 1936. MGM. Jack Conway. With Spencer Tracy, Myrna Loy, William Powell

Rita Hayworth

Unless otherwise stated, the production company was Columbia.

Only Angels Have Wings. 1939. Howard Hawks. With Cary Grant, Jean Arthur, Richard Barthelmess, Thomas Mitchell

Susan and God (The Gay Mrs Trexel). 1940. MGM. George Cukor. With Joan Crawford, Fredric March, Ruth Hussey, John Carroll, Nigel Bruce, Constance Collier

The Strawberry Blonde. 1941. Warner Bros. Raoul Walsh. With James Cagney, Olivia de Havilland, Alan Hale, Jack Carson

Blood and Sand. 1941. Twentieth Century-Fox. Rouben Mamoulian. With Tyrone Power, Linda Darnell, Nazimova, Laird Cregar

You Were Never Lovelier. 1942. William A. Seiter. With Fred Astaire, Adolphe Menjou, Larry Parks, Leslie Brooks, Isobel Elsom, Xavier Cugat and his Orchestra. [Rita Hayworth dubbed as singer]

Cover Girl. 1944. Charles Vidor. With Gene Kelly, Lee Bownan, Eve Arden, Otto Kruger, Jinx Falkenberg. [Rita Hayworth dubbed as singer]

Gilda. 1946. Charles Vidor. With Glenn Ford, George Macready, Gerald Mohr, Joseph Calleia

The Lady from Shanghai. 1948. Orson Welles. With Welles, Everett Sloane, Glenn Anders

Pal Joey. 1957. George Sidney. With Frank Sinatra, Kim Novak, Barbara Nichols

Separate Tables. 1958. Hecht-Hill-Lancaster for United Artists. Delbert Mann. With Burt Lancaster, Deborah Kerr, David Niven, Wendy Hiller, Gladys Cooper, Cathleen Nesbitt, Rod Taylor, Felix Aylmer

Vivien Leigh

Fire Over England. 1937. United Artists. Erich Pommer. With Flora Robson, Laurence Olivier

St Martin's Lane. 1938. Pommer. Tim Whelan. With Charles Laughton, Rex Harrison

Gone with the Wind. 1939.

MGM. Victor Fleming (initially, George Cukor). With Clark Gable, Olivia de Havilland, Leslie Howard

Lady Hamilton (That Hamilton Woman). 1941. United Artists. Alexander Korda. With Laurence Olivier

Caesar and Cleopatra. 1945. Rank. Gabriel Pascal. With Claude Rains, Stewart Granger, Jean Simmons, Flora Robson

A Streetcar named Desire. 1951. Warner Bros. Elia Kazan. With Marlon Brando, Kim Hunter

The Roman Spring of Mrs Stone. 1961. Warner Bros. José Quintero. With Warren Beatty, Lotte Lenya

Ship of Fools. 1965. Columbia. Stanley Kramer. With Simone Signoret, Jose Ferrer, Lee Marvin, Oscar Werner

Gina Lollobrigida

Les Belles de Nuit. 1952. René Clair. With Gérard Philipe, Madeleine Carol

La Provinciale. 1952. Mario Soldati. With Gabriele Ferzetti. [The first film in which Gina Lollobrigida's own voice was used]

Bread; Love and Dreams. 1953. Luigi Comencini. With Vittorio De Sica

La Romana. 1954. Luigi Zampa. With Daniel Gélin, Franco Fabrizi, Raymond Pellegrin

Bread, Love and Jealousy. 1954. Luigi Comencini. With Vittorio De Sica

Trapeze. 1956. Hecht-Lancaster for United Artists. Carol Reed. With Burt Lancaster, Tony Curtis

Solomon and Sheba. 1959. United Artists. King Vidor With Yul Brynner, George Sanders

Sophia Loren

L'Oro di Napoli. 1954. Pont De Laurentiis. Vittorio De Sica. With Toto, Silvana Mangano, Eduardo De Filippo

Desire Under the Elms. 195? Paramount. Delbert Mann. With Burl Ives, Anthony Perkins

The Key. 1958. Columbia. Carol Reed. With William Holden, Trevor Howard

It Started in Naples. 1960. Paramount. Melville Shavelson. With Clark Gable, Vittorio De Sica

Heller in Pink Tights. 1960. Paramount-Ponti. George Cukor. With Anthony Quinn, Margaret O'Brien, Ramon Novarro

Two Women (La Ciociara). 1961. Ponti. Vittorio De Sica. With Jean-Paul Belmondo, Raf Vallone. [Sophia Loren won an Osca for this film]

Boccaccio 70. [episode, *Le Riffa*, directed by Vittorio De Sica]. 1962

The Countess from Hong Kong. Universal. Charles Chaplin. With Marlon Brando

The Man of La Mancha. 1972. Arthur Hiller. With Peter O'Toole

Marilyn Monroe

Unless otherwise stated, the production company was Twentieth Century-Fox.

Love Happy. 1949. United Artists. David Miller. With the Marx Brothers

The Asphalt Jungle. 1950. MGM. John Huston. With Sterling Hayden, Louis Calhern

All About Eve. 1950. Joseph L. Mankiewicz. With Bette Davis, George Sanders, Anne Baxter, Gary Merrill

Love Nest. 1951. Joseph Newman. With June Haver, William Lundigan, Frank Fay

Clash by Night. 1952. RKO. Fritz Lang. With Barbara Stanwyck, Paul Douglas, Robert Ryan

e're not Married. 1952. Edmund Goulding. With Ginger Rogers, Fred Allen, Victor Moore, David Wayne, Eve Arden, Paul Douglas, Eddie Bracken, Mitzi Gaynor, Louis Calhern, Zsa Zsa Gabor

Monkey Business. 1952. Howard Hawks. With Cary Grant, Ginger Rogers, Charles Coburn

Full House. 1952. (Episode: The Cop and the Anthem)

Henry Koster. With Charles Laughton, David Wayne
Niagara. 1953. Henry Hathaway. With Joseph Cotten, Jean Peters
Gentlemen Prefer Blondes. 1953. Howard Hawks. With Jane Russell, Charles Coburn
How to Marry a Millionaire. 1953. Jean Negulesco. With Betty Grable, Lauren Bacall, David Wayne, William Powell
The Seven Year Itch. 1955. Billy Wilder. With Tom Ewell, Evelyn Keyes, Sonny Tufts
Bus Stop. 1956. Joshua Logan. With Don Murray, Arthur O'Connell, Betty Field
The Prince and the Showgirl. 1957. Warner Bros. Laurence Olivier. With Olivier, Sybil Thorndyke, Richard Wattis
Some Like It Hot. 1959. United Artists. Billy Wilder. With Tony Curtis, Jack Lemmon, George Raft, Pat O'Brien, Joe E. Brown
Let's Make Love. 1960. George Cukor. With Yves Montand, Frankie Vaughan
The Misfits. 1961. United Artists. John Huston. With Clark Gable, Montgomery Clift, Eli Wallach, Thelma Ritter

Jeanne Moreau
Touchez-pas au Grisby. 1954. Jacques Becker. With Jean Gabin, René Dary, Dora Doll
Ascenseur pour l'échafaud. 1957. Louis Malle. With Maurice Ronet, Yori Bertin, Georges Poujouly
Les Amants. 1958. Louis Malle. With Alain Cuny, Jean-Marc Bory

Les Liaisons Dangereuses. 1959. Roger Vadim. With Gérard Philipe, Annette Stroyberg, Jean-Louis Trintignant
Moderato Cantabile. 1960. Peter Brook. With Jean Paul Belmondo, Didier Haudepin
La Notte. 1961. Michelangelo Antonioni. With Marcello Mastroianni, Monica Vitti, Bernhard Wicki
Jules et Jim. 1961. François Truffaut. With Oscar Werner, Henri Serre
The Trial. 1962. Orson Welles. With Anthony Perkins, Orson Welles, Romy Schneider, Elsa Martinelli, Akim Tamiroff
Le Feu Follet. 1963. Louis Malle. With Maurice Ronet
Diary of a Chambermaid. 1964. Luis Buñuel. With Georges Géret, Michel Piccoli, Françoise Lugagne
Mata Hari, Agent H.21. 1964. Jean-Louis Richard. With Jean-Louis Trintignant
Viva Maria! 1965. Louis Malle. With Brigitte Bardot, George Hamilton
The Immortal Story. 1966/68. Orson Welles. With Orson Welles, Roger Coggio, Norman Eshley
Mademoiselle. 1966. Woodfall (London)/ Procinex (Rome). Tony Richardson. With Ettore Manni, Keith Skinner
The Sailor from Gibraltar. 1967. Woodfall. Tony Richardson. With Ian Bannen, Vanessa Redgrave, Orson Welles

La Mariée était en noir. 1967. François Truffaut. With Jean Claude Brialy

Mary Pickford
The Violin-Maker of Cremona. 1909. Biograph. D. W. Griffith. With John Compson, David Miles, Owen Moore
The Little Teacher. 1909. Biograph. D. W. Griffith. With Arthur Johnson
The New York Hat. 1912. Biograph. D. W. Griffith. With Lionel Barrymore, the Gish sisters, Robert Harron, Mae Marsh. (Anita Loos's first screenplay)
Tess of the Storm Country. 1914. Famous Players.

Edwin S. Porter. With Olive Fuller Gordon, David Wartford, Harold Lockwood
A Poor Little Rich Girl. 1917. Paramount. Maurice Tourneur. With Frank Andrews, Charles Craig, Madeleine Traverse, Charles Wellesly
Rebecca of Sunnybrook Farm. 1917. Paramount. Marshall Neilan (first film as director). With Wesley Barry, Majorie Daw, Mayme Kelso, Eugene O'Brien, Charles Ogle, ZaZu Pitts (first film)
Stella Maris. 1918. Artcraft. Marshall Neilan. With Joseph Crowell, Conway Tearle, Ida Waterman. (Dual role for Mary Pickford)
Daddy Long Legs. 1919. First National. Marshall Neilan. With Betty Banton, Wesley Barry, Milla Davenport, Mahlon Hamilton. (First film as producer for Mary Pickford)

Pollyanna. 1920. United Artists. Paul Powell. With George Berrell, William Courtleigh, Helen Jerome Eddy
Little Lord Fauntleroy. 1921. United Artists. Alfred E. Green and Jack Pickford. With Rose Dione, Joseph Dowling, Claude Gillingwater, Frances Marion
Coquette. 1929. United Artists. Sam Taylor. With Louise Beavers, John Mack Brown, George Irving, Matt Moore. (First sound film.) (Mary Pickford won an Academy Award as Best Actress)
The Taming of the Shrew. 1929 United Artists. Sam Taylor. With Douglas Fairbanks. (Also silent version; only film with Douglas Fairbanks)
Kiki. 1931. United Artists. Sam Taylor. With Reginald Denny, Margaret Livingston
Secrets. 1933. United Artists. Frank Borzage. With Leslie Howard

Gloria Swanson
Male and Female. 1919. Artcraft-Paramount. Cecil B. De Mille. With Thomas

Meighan, Lila Lee, Theodore Roberts, Bebe Daniels
Beyond the Rocks. 1922. Paramount. Sam Wood. With Rudolf Valentino
My American Wife. 1923. Paramount. Sam Wood. With Antonio Moreno
Manhandled. 1924. Paramount. Allan Dwan. With Tom Moore, Frank Morgan
Madame Sans-Gêne. 1925. Paramount. (made in France). Leonce Perret. With Emile Drain, Charles DeRoche, Warwick Ward
Sadie Thompson (Somerset Maugham's 'Rain'). 1928. United Artists. Raoul Walsh. With Lionel Barrymore, Blanche Frederici
Queen Kelly. 1928. United Artists. Erich von Stroheim. With Walter Byron, Seena Owen
Perfect Understanding. 1933. United Artists. Cyril Gardiner. With Laurence Olivier, John Halliday, Nigel Playfair, Nora Swinburne
Sunset Boulevard. 1950. Paramount. Billy Wilder. With William Holden, Erich von Stroheim, Nancy Olson, Jack Webb, H. B. Warner (supporting), Buster Keaton, Hedda Hopper, Cecil B. De Mille

Elizabeth Taylor
National Velvet. 1944. MGM. Clarence Brown, With Mickey Rooney, Donald Crisp
A Place in the Sun. 1951. Paramount. George Stevens. With Montgomery Clift, Raymond Burr, Shelley Winters

Raintree Country. 1957.
MGM. Edward Dmytryk.
With Montgomery Clift, Eva
Marie Saint, Nigel Patrick,
Lee Marvin, Agnes
Moorehead

Cat on a Hot Tin Roof. 1958.
Richard Brooks. With Paul
Newman, Burl Ives, Judith
Anderson, Jack Carson

Suddenly Last Summer.
1959. MGM. Joseph L.
Mankiewicz. With
Katharine Hepburn,
Montgomery Clift

Butterfield 8. 1960. MGM.
Daniel Mann. With

Laurence Harvey.
[Elizabeth Taylor won an
Oscar for this film]

Cleopatra. 1963. Twentieth
Century-Fox. Joseph L.
Mankiewicz. With Rex
Harrison, Richard Burton,
Roddy MacDowall, Hume
Cronym, Robert Stephens

The VIPs. 1964. Anthony
Asquith. With Richard
Burton, Louis Jourdain,
Elsa Martinelli, Margaret
Rutherford, Maggie Smith,
Rod Taylor, Orson Welles,
Linda Christian, Dennis
Price

The Sandpiper. 1965. MGM/
Filmways. Vincente
Minnelli. With Richard
Burton, Eva Marie Saint

*Who's Afraid of Virginia
Woolf?* 1966. Warners. Mike
Nichols. With Richard
Burton, George Segal, Sandy
Dennis. [Elizabeth Taylor
won her second Oscar]

The Taming of the Shrew.
1967. Columbia. Franco
Zefferelli. With Richard
Burton

Reflections in a Golden Eye.
1967. Warner Brothers/
Seven Arts. John Huston.

With Marlon Brando, Brian
Keith, Julie Harris

Boom! 1968. World Film
Service/Moon Lake
Productions. Joseph Losey.
With Richard Burton, Noël
Coward, Joanna Shimkus

Secret Ceremony. 1968.
Universal/World Films/Paul
M. Heller. Joseph Losey.
With Mia Farrow, Robert
Mitchum, Pamela Bruce,
Peggy Ashcroft

The Only Game in Town.
1969. Twentieth Century-
Fox. George Stevens. With
Warren Beatty

SELECTED BIBLIOGRAPHY

Arletty. 'Strictly Entre
Nous.' *Penguin Film
Review*, No. 7. London,
Penguin Books, 1948

Armes, Roy. *French Cinema
since 1946.* Vols I and II.
London, Tantivy Press,
revised, 1970

Bainbridge, John. *Garbo.*
London, Frederick Muller,
1955.

Beauvoir, Simone de.
*Brigitte Bardot and the
Lolita Syndrome.* London,
Andre Deutsch/Weidenfeld
and Nicolson, 1960; New
English Library, 1962

Blum, Daniel. *A Pictorial
History of the Silent Screen.*
Originally pub. 1953;
reissued London, Hamlyn,
1962 and 1973

Blum, Daniel. *A Pictorial
History of the Talkies.*
London, Spring Books, 1958

Brownlow, Kevin. *The
Parade's Gone By.* New
York, Alfred A. Knopf, 1968

Carr, Larry. *Four Fabulous
Faces* [Gloria Swanson,
Greta Garbo, Joan
Crawford, Marlene
Dietrich]. New Rochelle,
NY, Arlington House

Crawford, Joan (in
collaboration with Jane
Kesner Ardmore). *A
Portrait of Joan.* New York,
Doubleday and Co., 1962

D'Arcy, Susan. *The Films of
Elizabeth Taylor.* London,
Barndon Castell Williams
Ltd, 1974

Davies, Dentner. *Jean
Harlow – Hollywood Comet.*
London, Constable, 1937

Durgnat, Raymond and
Kobal, John. *Greta Garbo.*
London, Studio Vista, 1965

Frewin, Leslie. *Dietrich.*
London, Frewin, 1967.
(Revision of *Blonde Venus*,
1955)

Griffith, D.W. *The Man who
Invented Hollywood; the
Autobiography of D.W.
Griffith.* Edited by James
Hart. Louisville, Touchstone
Publishing Co., 1972

Griffith, Mrs D.W. (Linda
Arvidson). *When the Movies
were Young.* Originally
published 1925. Revised and
reissued by Dover
Publications, Toronto, 1969

Griffith, Richard and Mayer,
Arthur. *The Movies.* New
York, Simon and Schuster,
1957

Guiles, Fred Laurence.
*Norma Jean: a Life of
Marilyn Monroe.* London,
W.H. Allen, 1969;
Mayflower, 1971

Hoyt, Edwin P. *The Tragic
Venus.* New York, Duell,
Sloan and Pearce, 1965

Jacobs, Lewis. *The Rise of
the American Film.* New
York, Harcourt Brace and
Co., 1939

Kobal, John. *Marlene
Dietrich.* London, Studio
Vista, 1968

Kobal, John. 'Rita
Hayworth.' *Focus on Film*,
No. 10. London, Tantivy
Press, 1972

Kobal, John. *Marilyn
Monroe.* London, Hamlyn
Publishing Company, 1974

Laborderie, Renaud de.
Brigitte Bardot. London,
World Distributors, 1964

Lambert, Gavin. *On Cukor.*
New York, Putnam's Sons,
1972

Lawton, Richard. *The
Image-Maker: Sixty Years of
Hollywood Glamour.*
London, Octopus, 1973

Lawton, Richard and
Leckey, Hugo. *Grand
Illusions.* London, Octopus,
1973

Mailer, Norman. *Marilyn.*
London, Hodder and
Stoughton, 1973; New York,
Grosset and Dunlop, 1973

Manvell, Roger (Chief
Editor). *International
Encyclopedia of Film.* New
York, Crown, 1972; London,
Michael Joseph, 1972

Marguerite, Yves. *Brigitte
Bardot.* Paris, Vedettes du
Cinéma, N.D. [*c.* 1962]

Mellen, Joan. *Marilyn
Monroe.* New York,
Pyramid, 1973

Morin, Edgar. *The Stars.*
Evergreen Profile Book.
London, John Calder, 1960;
New York, Grove Press, 1960

Parrish, James Robert. *The
Fox Girls.* New Rochelle,
NY, Arlington House, 1971

Parrish, James Robert. *The
Paramount Pretties.* New
Rochelle, NY, Arlington
House, 1972

Pickford, Mary. *Sunshine
and Shadow.* New York,
Doubleday, 1955

Powdermaker, Hortense.
*Hollywood, the Dream
Factory.* London, Secker and
Warburg, 1951

Quirk, Laurence J. *The
Films of Ingrid Bergman.*
New York, Citadel Press,
1970

Ramsay, Terry. *A Million
and One Nights.* New York,
Simon and Schuster, 1926

Robyns, Gwen. *Light of a
Star: Vivien Leigh.* London,
Leslie Frewin, 1968

Rosten, Leo. *Hollywood.*
New York, Harcourt Brace
and Co., 1941

Selznick, David O. *Memo
from: David O. Selznick.*
The Viking Press, 1972.
Avon Paperback, 1973

Shipman, David. *The Great
Movie Stars – the Golden
Years.* London, Hamlyn
Publishing Co., 1970

Shipman, David. *The Great
Movie Stars – the
International Years.* London,
Angus and Robertson, 1972

Shulman, Irving. *Harlow.*
New York, Dell Publishing
Co. 1964

Slide, Anthony. *The Griffith
Actresses.* London, Tantivy
Press, 1973

Sternberg, Josef von. *Fun in
a Chinese Laundry.* London,
Secker and Warburg, 1965

Taylor, Elizabeth. *Elizabeth
Taylor, an Informal Memoir.*
New York, Harper and Row,
1965

Taylor, John Russell, and
Jackson, Arthur. *The
Hollywood Musical.* London,
Secker and Warburg, 1971

Thorp, Margaret Farrand.
America at the Movies. New
Haven, Yale University
Press, 1939

Walker, Alexander. *The
Celluloid Sacrifice.* London,
Michael Joseph, 1966;
reissued as *Sex in the
Movies*, by Penguin Books

Walker, Alexander.
*Stardom, the Hollywood
Phenomenon.* London,
Michael Joseph, 1970.
Reissued by Penguin Books,
1974

Wanger, Walter and Hyams,
Joe. *My Life with Cleopatra.*
London, Bantam/Corgi, 1963

Windeler, Robert.
*Sweetheart: the Story of
Mary Pickford.* London,
W.H. Allen, 1973

World Encyclopedia of Film.
November Books/Studio
Vista, London, 1972

Zukor, Adolph. *The Public is
Never Wrong.* London,
Cassell, 1974

Acknowledgements

The pictures in this book are from the author's collection,
from the collections of John Kobal and Ronald Grant,
and from the Hamlyn Group Library.

In addition to the above, the publishers acknowledge
with thanks the production companies and distributors
associated with the films: Chadwick, Columbia,
Cosmopolitan, Embassy, Fox, Gala, London Films,
Lopert, MGM, Paramount, Pommer, J. Arthur Rank,
RKO, Sofar Film, Svensk Filmindustri, Times,
Twentieth Century-Fox, UFA, United Artists, Universal,
Warner Brothers, Warner-7 Arts, Woodfall, Zenith.

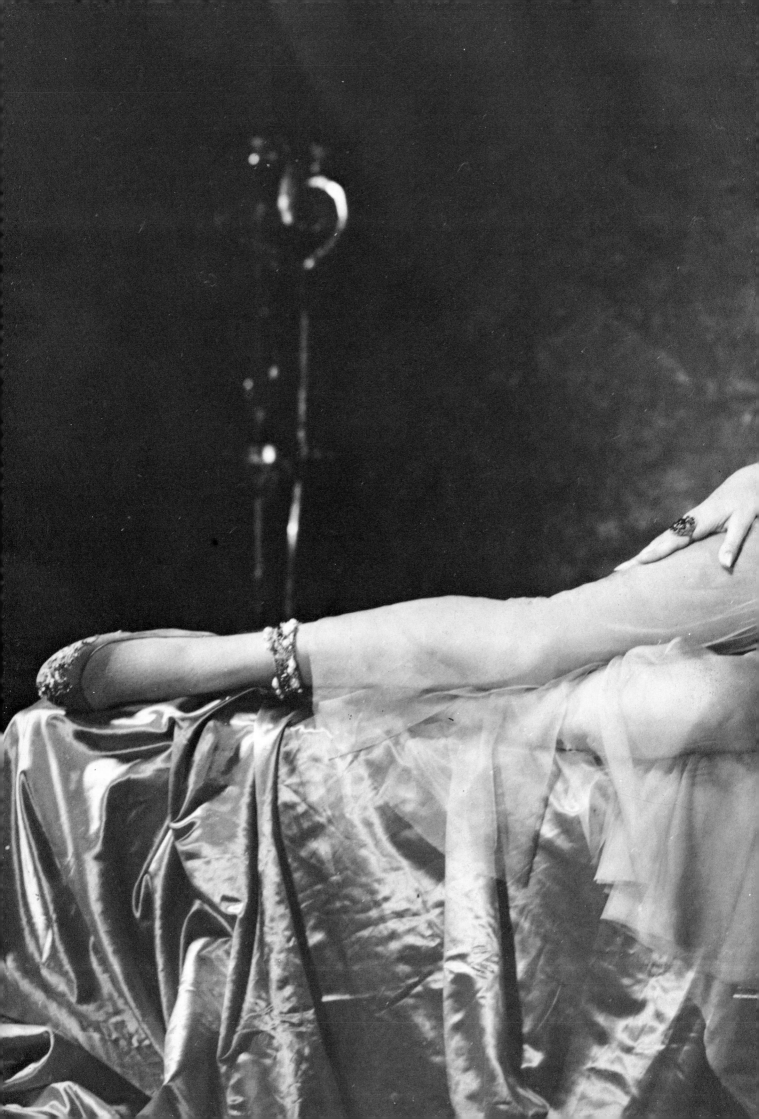